MACEDONIA: A HISTORY

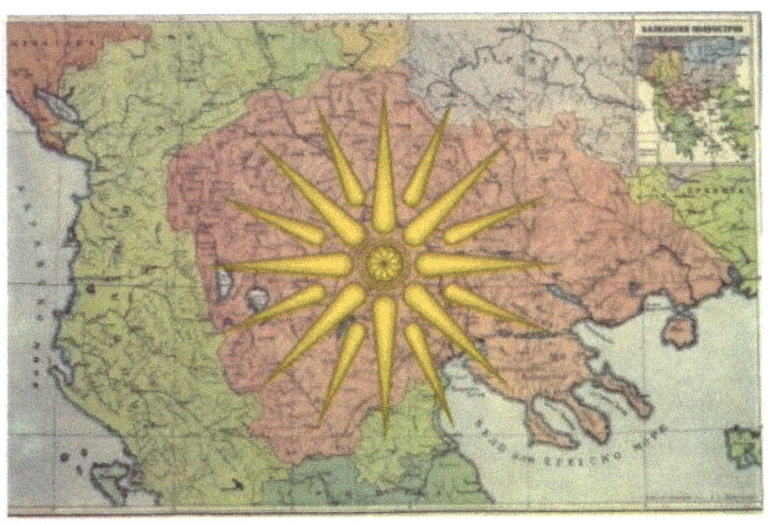

Published By Simon Tasievski

2025

Simon Tasievski

Macedonia: A History

Simon Tasievski

TABLE OF CONTENTS

FOREWORD	6
HISTORICAL REFERENCES BY AUTHORS BOTH ANCIENT AND CONTEMPORARY	12
IMPORTANT POINTS OF REFERENCE	16
GODS	26
GREEK OR MACEDONIAN I	28
HOMER	34
GREEK OR MACEDONIAN II	36
NONSENSICAL MIGRATION THEORY WHICH HAS NEVER BEEN PROVEN AND REJECTED AS FACT.	58
MACEDONIA DURING BYZANTIAN RULE	66
IMPORTANT REFERENCES	70
KALASH & THE HUNZA	78
POLITICS, OFFICIAL NAME CHANGES, FORCIBLE INTEGRATION, AND ANNEXATION OF LANDS	90
MAP DISPLAYING THE VILLAGES AND TOWN NAME CHANGES.	112

THE ROSETTA STONE	126
THE NAME DISPUTE	134
BIBLICAL REFERENCES TO MACEDONIA	146
BIBLICAL REFERENCES:	148
NEWSPAPER ARTICLES REFERRING TO MACEDONIA 1814 – 1947 AND BEYOND	154
REGARDING ENTRY TO NATO, THE EU AND THE UN	206
CONCLUSION	208
THERE CANNOT BE AN ANCIENT VERSION OF A MODERN COUNTRY, IT'S AS SIMPLE AS THAT.	210
ACKNOWLEDGEMENTS	214
RECOMMENDED & SUGGESTED READING – ALL AVAILABLE IN E-BOOK AND MOSTLY FOR FREE BY THESE AUTHORS	216

FOREWORD

My name is Simon Tasievski, I am an Australian born descendent of Macedonian heritage.

Having a bordering obsessive interest in both geography and ancient history, I have studied and researched both of these subjects at length; Macedonia in particular for well over 25 years, eager to understand and feel a closer connection to my ancestral homeland that is filled with an abundance of history. A place where my grandfathers, grandfathers, grandfathers came from.

I am a proud Australian, I love this country and always will, it is and always will be my home. But as any Australian with European heritage and a fascination with ancient history, there will always be a soft spot in my heart which is only natural.

For many people, the name Macedonia brings to them a patriotic feeling of warmth, a connection to a land with thousands of years of history. A land of hero's, a land of sorrows, a land of both heartache and love. A country within the heart of Europe that has experienced the very highest of highs as well as the lowest of lows. A country that has at times been the conqueror, and one that was eventually conquered itself.

As the world around us constantly evolves and changes over time, there is certainly no shortage of those that will always want to take that away from us, however, the very words of the authors both ancient and contemporary seem to contradict what modern states and trolls attempt to claim.

Now, I want to make it absolutely clear that there are both good and bad people of every single nationality on Earth and from all walks of life. This is not an attack on any one particular nation or people. I have friends from all different nationalities. One of my best friends is a Greek and I have many other Greek friends! They understand history as well as my knowledge of the subject and there is and always be a mutual respect between us. However, there currently exist and will always be the uninformed and uneducated trolls out there foolishly attempting to tear others down so this is aimed directly at them. I will just let the facts speak for themselves to easily tear apart their nonsense.

We often hear, "Macedonia doesn't exist", "Macedonia is Greek and has always been Greek", "You are all Slavs that arrived in the 6th century", "You are Bulgarian", "Macedonia means "tall man/person in Greek"" (By the way I challenge anyone to show me how or where, anywhere, that the word Macedonia translates into *tall man anything* in both either ancient or modern Greek (which is in fact Koine and not even 'Greek' to begin with at all, that is discussed at length in this book), as you will not find it translates to that anywhere in any possible variation or form)) etc. from those without an iota of knowledge and those that have done absolutely zero research into the subject. It appears that it is much easier for them to simply parrot what they have been told to say as well as evidently be incapable of thinking and researching any actual facts for themselves.

This book places all of those false claims to rest once and for all - never to be repeated again as I will have just destroyed that absolute nonsense right here and now in these very pages.

Over time I have collected hundreds of books, papers, manuscripts, and thousands of documents to educate myself on what is true and what is false. When someone makes a claim, I never take this at face value and actually look into their statement to see if I am correct, or if I was wrong. In the past I often refuted the claims with factual evidence, references, and sources, but instead of addressing what I had stated, they will often just ignore the facts and sources then throw another meaningless and pointless insult my way.

It became a vicious cycle that gets nowhere and becomes a complete waste of time; falling on deaf ears, and to date, I have never, not once had a single person be able to answer or refute the facts as I had presented to them.

So, what I did was note down these sources, these authors, these historians from both past and present, and then compile them into a manuscript for easy navigation. It occurred to me that with the sheer volume of knowledge and evidence that I had collected, that perhaps I should share this knowledge and research with the millions of people and especially, those of Macedonian descent from around the world.

This book has been compiled as a collection of facts and statements in an easy-to-read format, with references to the author, the newspaper clipping, the publication, the document, the biblical reference, the dates, that refute any and all false claims as to the legitimacy of the Macedonian State that has existed for well over 4,000 years, long before any of the modern neighboring countries or names of those countries had ever existed.

Was it not George Santayana in 1905 who said: "Those who cannot remember the past are condemned to repeat it", and *not* as was previously believed Winston Churchill, who simply paraphrased him (George Santayana) later on in 1948 has received the recognition for that saying ever since.

A perfect example of how one thing can simply be repeated over and over again but does not detract from the truth that it was never his saying to begin with at all.

What I hope to achieve with this book is quite simple. There are already thousands of books in existence on both ancient as well as on Macedonian history. I own and have read many of them, and as you can imagine; many are factually incorrect spreading false narratives for their own benefit. However, none are anything like what I have developed here. It is structured in a format that I have still not yet seen to date. Something that is easy to read and more importantly, easy for anyone to reference back to with ease.

In the world we have both readers and non-readers. This book will help bridge that gap due to the format I had designed it for, getting the knowledge and information across to those who want and need it the most; and to those who wouldn't ordinarily ever pick up and read a thick novel.

When the subject of history is ever brought up, I have often found that it is fairly easy for me to command silence and respect in the room as people actually listen. This can only ever happen when one has a profound and unencumbered knowledge of the subject which I take great pride in.

There are only 3 countries in the world today that have never been known as anything other than that which they are known as today since prehistory. These 3 countries are Egypt, which has always been Egypt. China, which has always been China, and Macedonia. Macedonia has always been Macedonia. (There is no "North" Macedonia. How can there be when there is no such thing as a "South" Macedonia?)

Concerning Macedonia's immediate neighbours, that being Serbia, Greece, Bulgaria and Albania, quite simply didn't exist and not only in prehistoric times but even within the last few hundred years.

All ancient maps already prove this.

Modern Serbia in ancient times was always known as Illyria. Serbia only became a country in 1878.

Modern Greece was always only ever a disconnected collection of City States where over 30 different and unintelligible languages between them were spoken (more on the Koine language later in the book), often cited as either Achea or Morea on all ancient maps only became a country in 1830.

Modern Bulgaria was always known as Thrace. Bulgaria only became a country in 1870.

Modern Albania was always known as Epirus. Albania only became a country in 1912.

Now Macedonia, both ancient and modern, has always been known as the country of Macedonia which those very same ancient maps illustrate quite clearly.

From Homeric to modern times, Macedonia has always existed.

I hope that you read and enjoy this book that has taken me decades to collect all of the information on, so that we can collectively as a refined, cultivated society, correct the mistakes of the past, rewrite the factually incorrect history books, and *finally* put to rest any and all false claims that could and have ever possibly be presented to you.

Simon Tasievski

My grandfather – Zivko Tasievski (my father's father). Born 1915. Died 1997.

Selo (Village) Logovardi, Bitola, Macedonia.

Simon Tasievski

HISTORICAL REFERENCES BY AUTHORS BOTH ANCIENT AND CONTEMPORARY

There are numerous historians, authors and orators from all around the world, coming from many different ethnicities all confirming and referring to Macedonia as a separate country from what the city states (which is what we today call the modern state of Greece) and surrounding countries were. To name just a few:

Aeschines

Agnes Savil

Andronikos

Apollodori

Aristotel

Arrian

Callisthenes

Carl Hron

Curtius Rufus

Demosthenes

Dimitrakos

Diodorus Siculus

Eratosthenes

Ernst Badian

Fon Stoutenberg

F.W. Wallbank

George Grote

Hatzidakis

Herodotus

Hesiodus

Homer

Iakovakis Rizos Nerulos

Isocrates

Professor James A. Harrison

Josephus

Lycurgus

Mpampiniotis

Nicholas Hammond

Papastavrou

Paul Cartledge

Paul Theroux

Pauzania

Pausanias

Pierre Jouguet

Philocrates

Plutarch

Polybius

Pompeius Throgus,

Quintus Rufus

Robert A. Hudley

Sakelariou

Strabo

Thycudides

Viperids

Wilcken's

Winston Churchill

Yerasimos Kaklamanis

Demosthenes was an ancient Hellenic philosopher and orator. What made him that known and famous as he is today are his "Phililpiki" - speeches against Philip II of Macedon and his barbarous Macedonians.

"That man Philip, not only he is not a Hellen, but also he does not have anything in common with the Hellenes. If only he would have been a barbarian from a decent country - but he is not even that. He is a scabby creature from Macedonia - a land that one can not even bring a slave that is worth something from."

* *'Barbarian' in ancient Greek means 'foreigner', 'non-greek'*

ALWAYS REMEMBER: "Phillip II, Alexander the Great and Aristotle were Macedonians."

"Cyril and Methodie were Macedonians."

"The Macedonians are not Slavic."

"The Macedonians are not Greek."

Dedicated to the untold numbers of Macedonians who perpetuate their glorious Macedonian heritage.

W. E. Gladstone

"MACEDONIA — FOR THE MACEDONIANS"
(William Gladstone in the House of Commons 1897)
Text of W. E. Gladstone's letter to the Byron Society for aid to Christians.

"Harwarden Castle."
January 1st, 1897.

IMPORTANT POINTS OF REFERENCE

No ancient maps ever show a "Greece" nor will they, for that region as the modern country of Greece was only first conceived in 1830. Neither was Bulgaria a country until after 1870.

They simply weren't countries prior to these dates.

Modern Greece was always only ever a collection of city states. What we today call Greece proper is marked as Achaea. Bulgaria was always known as Thrace. Serbia was always known as Illyria. Albania was always known as Epirus. However, Macedonia was always Macedonia on ancient maps as well as modern.

These maps will however show "Morea" on all ancient maps, which is the current Peloponnesus region at the far southern tip surrounded by the Mediterranean Sea within the modern-day state of Greece. The Macedonian word for sea is "More" (Mo-re).

So, it is rather interesting to note that there is a Macedonian word in place for a land that is surrounded by the "sea" wouldn't you agree?

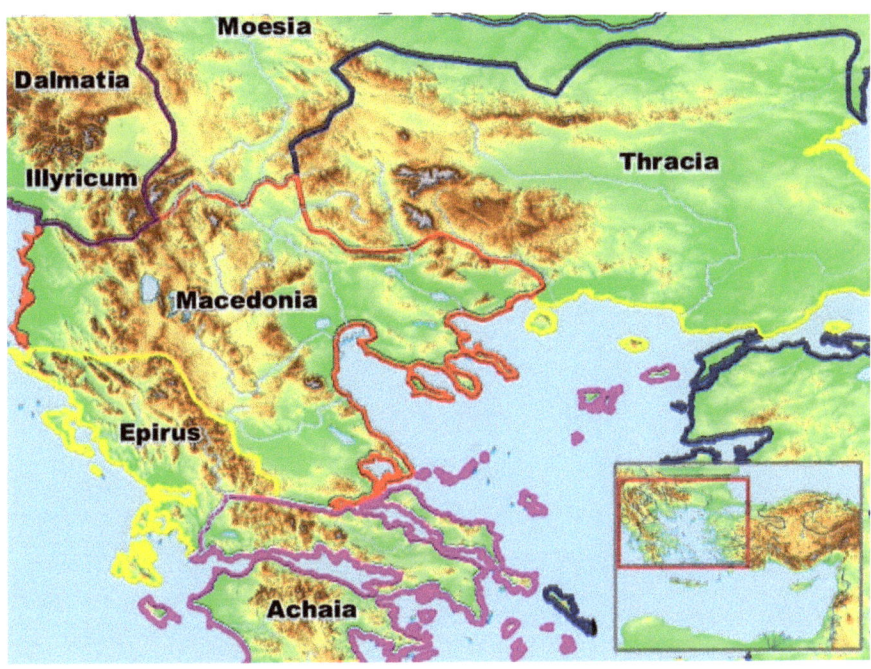

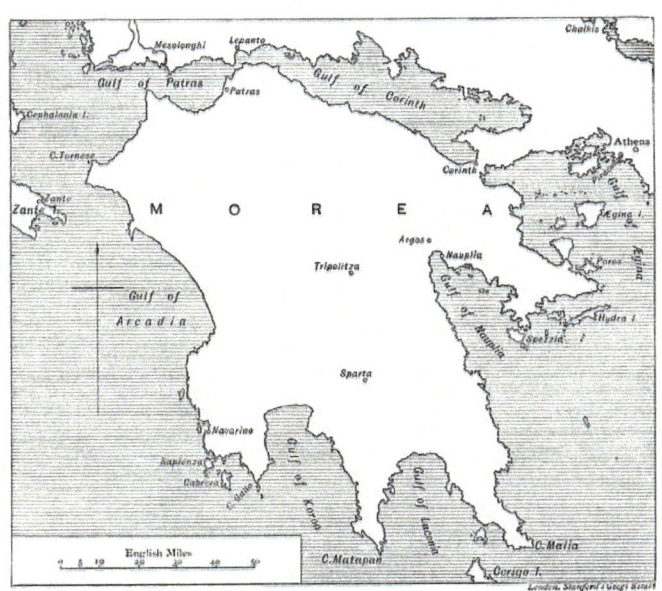

Simon Tasievski

The Holy Bible is over 2,000 years old. Macedonia is directly mentioned in the Holy Bible 27 times and numerous more times indirectly, whereas the words 'Greece' or 'Hellas' referenced as a country is never mentioned not even once (as it didn't exist back then – only since 1830). What the Jews in ancient times within the Holy Bible called "Greeks", meant for anyone living north of the Mediterranean Sea on the continent of Europe whether it be (for modern) Turkey, Switzerland, Italy or Spain.

Every non-Jew from anywhere on the continent of Europe was called a 'Greek'.
For the non-Jews living in the Middle East - they were called Gentiles.
(note the separations and see further on chapter for Biblical references to Macedonia).

> Romans 15 | KJV
>
> saints. [26] For it hath pleased them of Macedonia and Achaia to make a certain contribution for the poor saints which are at Jerusalem. [27] It hath pleased them verily; and their debtors they are. For if the Gentiles have been made partakers of their spiritual things, their duty is also to minister unto them in carnal things. [28] When therefore I have performed this, and have sealed to them this fruit, I will come by you into Spain. [29] And I am sure that, when I come unto you, I shall come in the fulness of the blessing of the gospel of Christ.

> **1 Thessalonians 1** NIV
>
> You became imitators of us and of the Lord, for you welcomed the message in the midst of severe suffering with the joy given by the Holy Spirit. And so you became a model to all the believers in <u>Macedonia and Achaia</u>. The Lord's message rang out from you <u>not only in Macedonia and Achaia</u>—your faith in God has become known everywhere. Therefore we do not need to say anything about it, for they themselves report what kind of reception you gave us. They tell how you turned to God from idols

> **Acts 20** KJV
>
> ## Macedonia
>
> And after the uproar was ceased, Paul called unto *him* the disciples, and embraced *them*, <u>and departed for to go into Macedonia</u>. And when he had gone over those parts, and had given them much

It is well established that Pella, founded by Filip II – King of Macedonia was the Macedonian Capital city in ancient times.
You can only ever have a capital city of a country. There is and has **never** been a 'city' there or anywhere in the region named "Macedonia", so when people say, "Macedonia was a city-state of Greece", that clearly makes no sense at all and to add to this, Macedonia was always ruled by a monarchy, whereas all the city-states took pride in being "democratic" and governed via a democracy (which was actually established and run by the Phoenicians (modern day Lebanon) centuries before it ever became popular in the city-state region).

Clearly the two systems are directly opposed to one another and **not** the same thing.

The city-states were appointed exactly as they were named – a 'state' that was named based around a specific 'city'. Athenians came from Athens. Spartans came from Sparta. Thebans came from Thebes. Corinthians came from Corinth.
All of these were cities.
So, to imply as the modern Greeks do that "Macedonia was a city-state of Greece!" is completely nonsensical. There was no city named Macedonia, and no country named Greece.

GODS

The common and modern misconception is that there is no such thing as 'Greek' gods per se, only 'ancient gods'. To name a few:

Greeks say Heracles, Romans say Hercules, Norse say Thor.
Greeks say Dionysus, Romans say Bacchus, Norse say Odin.
Greeks say Eros, Romans say Cupid, Norse say Aengus.
Greeks say Artemis, Romans say Diana, Norse say Skadi.
Greeks say Zeus, Romans say Jupiter, Norse also say Odin.
Greeks say Ares, Romans say Mars, Norse say Freyja.
Greeks say Hera, Romans say Juno, Norse say Frigg.
Greeks say Poseidon, Romans say Neptune, Norse say Njordr and Aesir.
Greeks say Athena, Romans say Minerva, Norse say Snotra, Sága.
Greeks say Cronos, Romans say Saturn, Norse say Njord.
Greeks say Hades, Romans say Pluto, Norse say Loki.
Greeks say Persephone, Romans say Proserpina, Norse say Hel.
Greeks say Aphrodite, Romans say Venus, Norse also say Freya.

All of Europe in ancient times **believed these exact same gods** with either the same name/very similar, or sometimes being called completely different, however, they are referred to as being one and the same.
This doesn't make them 'Greek' in any possible way, so people need to stop using this outdated and archaic phrase as god's don't have 'nationalities', nor are they 'born' in a specific country whether such countries existed or not.

In English we say God. In Hebrew it's Yaw Weh. In Arabic it's Allah.

Greek Name	Roman Name	Role
Zeus	Jupiter	King of the Gods, god of the Sky and Weather
Hera	Juno	Goddess of Marriage
Poseidon	Neptune	God of the Sea, Earthquakes and Horses
Demeter	Ceres	Goddess of Agriculture and Grain
Hestia	Vesta	Goddess of the Hearth and Home
Aphrodite	Venus	Goddess of Love and Beauty
Hephaestus	Vulcan	God of Metalworking and Fire
Ares	Mars	God of War and Battlelust
Hermes	Mercury	God of Messengers, Trade and Thieves
Apollo	Apollo	God of Music, Prophecy and Healing
Athena	Minerva	Goddess of Wisdom, War and Craft
Artemis	Diana	Goddess of Hunting, Animals and Children
Dionysus	Bacchus	God of Wine and Festivity
Heracles	Hercules	Apotheosised hero, Physical defender of Mount Olympus

GREEK OR MACEDONIAN I

It has been well documented that Philip II (father of Alexander the Great) was always referred to as a Philhellene which in Koine means 'friend of the Hellenes', and that Ptolemy Alorus as a guardian of Perdiccas and Philip was ruling until 365 B.C, when Perdiccas III came to the throne and liberated Philip who had been held as a hostage within the city-states.

Now why would Greeks hold their own people hostage, especially those of royal bloodlines which they themselves didn't have - as they were governed via democracies - if he were indeed a Greek himself?

Later, the new ruler (Philip) set up good relations with Thebes and therefore he was proclaimed "proxenos" and "evergetes" which in Koine means "friend and benefactor".
So, can someone please explain how can you officially be called a "friend of your own people" if they were all 'Greeks' themselves to begin with? This makes absolutely no sense.

Macedonia had always been ruled by a monarchy for well over 3 centuries even prior to King Philip II, whereas *all* the city-states were governed under a democracy (having no Kings or Queens in lieu of a politically democratic form of government for each city-state).
How could Macedonia and the city-states possibly somehow be the same thing?

Modern Greece loves to boast about being the "inventors" of democracy (among other things - even though a democratic form of governance i.e. democracy was *actually* first used by the Phoenicians many centuries earlier).

These city-states were referred to as being a "polis" which is where the word "politician" comes from; but we clearly have a distinct line of monarchy rule for hundreds of years all throughout Macedonia right up to and even well after 168 B.C, when Rome's conquests took place with Macedonia being the very last country to fall to Rome.

Their own words (polis and politician) automatically nullify their very own argument!

Democracy for the city-states is documented multiple times as being suppressed by the Macedonians, which was another reason why they hated the Macedonians so much and called them barbarians.

Simon Tasievski

Alexander III (the Great) had garrisons placed all throughout the city-states after he was crowned King of Macedonia. Not one to state the obvious here but garrisons never exist in your "own" country - which doesn't make any sense as they are only ever utilised in *conquered* territories.

The reason they (the city-statesmen) were rebelling is because they all hated the Macedonians, referring to them as barbarians which in the Koine language means foreigner.

Before his Asian campaign (the spring of 334 B.C) Alexander made an appeal to the city-states to refrain from any rebellions or attempted mutinies in his absence. The Greek (city-state) soldiers within Alexanders campaign were hostages as much as they were allies for their untoward behaviour and as an assurance that there would be no revolt in his absence. Despite this, rebellions arose on the island of Rhodes as well as in Sparta rejecting all military and political agreements with Alexander, who then established contacts with the leaders of the Persian Fleet.

Now why would he do this if they were as the Greeks attempt to claim all the same people i.e. Greeks?

It's simple because they weren't! Which also explains the rebellions, cheers, and revolts from every single one of the city-states upon the news of Alexanders death (which was only a false rumour as it hadn't actually happened as yet), and then cheered and tried to rebel once again when the news broke out that he had in fact died in Babylon in 323 B.C.

The ridiculous claim that Alexander "was Greek" because he competed in the Olympic Games is an outright absurdity. He was a King who had *conquered* the city-states and simply

decided that he was going to compete. Who was going to stop him and why? One, the city-states literally had no choice in the matter as they were conquered by war and by force, and two, the original border between Macedonia and the city-states (technically Thessaly) was Mount Olympus.
Mountain ranges are generally the border line between nations especially throughout Europe.

Macedonia: A History

HOMER

Alexander always carried with him a copy of The Iliad by Homer which apparently never left his side, nor did he ever go anywhere without it.

It is particularly interesting to note that there are multiple references with the words used in the original works of Homer, that are similarly close to (if not exactly the same) as modern Macedonian words, that I might also add are nothing at all similar to both modern or ancient Greek (Koine).

Macedonia: A History

Moderen English	Moderen Greek	Moderen Macedonian	HOMER
Greeting (hello)	Gyasu	Zdravo	Dravikos
Dear	Prosfilis	Mili	Mili
Possesive-own	Ktitos	Svoi	Svos
With	Me	So	Sun
Shake	Dono, Seio	Tresi	Tresi
Wood	Ksilo	Drvo	Druos
Madness/rage	Apotomos, parafron, trelos	Luta(female), lut(male)	Luta
Here	Edo	Ovde	Ode
Lay, put to bed	palagase, stroma	Legni, leglo	Leglo
Come on	Lipon	Ajde	Aijde
To remember	Min Ksexnas	Pamti	Pamti(s)
Song	Tragudao, traguda	Pesma, Pesna	Asma, Ejsma
To keep to hold	Sto hari	Vo raka	Eruko
In good spirit	Kalos	Aren	Arin
To beat by force	Derno, Dernis, Derni	Biya, Bie	Biya, Bie
My proof	Apadoksis	Dokaz moy	Doko moi
Knowing, skilfull	Eksipnos	ITRI(plural), Itar(single)	Idri
Journey, trip, walking	Vadizi, Ekdromi	Odi, odenye, od	Odeia
Bake	Pisisimo	Pechi	Pecko
Something sayed	(to) Ipan	Recheno	Recos
Speaking a passage	(to) Ipe	Recheno	Reces
To contair/cover	Sfingi	Stega	Stego
Tp Rub	Yaleyfo	Trie	Trio
Groaning	Vongizi	Stenka	Steno
Baren(old)	Agonos	Staro	Stero
To advance in speps(Lead)	Serni, Liveray	Vodi	Vadino
To Streach	Travay	Tegni	Teino
Glory, Miracle	Thavma	Chudo	Kudo
Dog	Skili	Kuche	Kuon
Eye	Mati, oftalmos	Oko	Okkos
the two eyes	Mataja, oftalmi	Oche	Ochi
Small cub	Levis	Kotle	Kotule
No	Ohi	Ne	Me
If	Ean	Ako	Ayke
Mother	Mitera	Mayka	Maya
He, Him	Aftos	Toy	Tu
Mine	Dikomu	Moi, moy	Moi
Spark	Spotha	Iskra	Iska'a
Brother-in-law	Yinikadelfos	Dever	Daer

GREEK OR MACEDONIAN II

Like many other authors of modern research, we believe that "Macedonianism" began with Philip II (359 B.C – 336 B.C) and lasted until 30 A.D when Cleopatra VII the Macedonian queen of Egypt – a descendent of Ptolemy I Soter who was one of Alexander the Great's generals, was defeated by Octavian when Egypt was subsequently conquered by Rome.

This means that the Macedonians dominated the then known world for well over 329 years. But can we truly say that Macedonian culture ended with the conclusion of Macedonian rule? No, because there were signs all throughout Roman and later Byzantine rule of an existence and continuation of a Macedonian culture. Alexander in his short career, had founded at least 33 cities which he named Alexandria (and not Alexandroupolis just to be clear). These cities and their Macedonian administrations and institutions continued to exist and function many generations after Macedonian rule had ended.

The most prominent of the Alexandria's founded by Alexander is Alexandria in Egypt. This is where the architect Dinokrit who had approached Alexander said: "I am Dinokrit, an architect from Macedonia and here I have plans and designs for a city worthy of Thy glory..." and Dinokrit delivered exactly what he had promised. A magnificent lighthouse was built near Alexandria on Farr Island, standing 110 metres tall. This was the great grandfather of all future lighthouses, which could be seen from a distance of 60 kilometres and was later dubbed as the "seventh wonder of the world".

Also built in Alexandria were the famous library and museum, the brain children of Alexander the Great. (Wilken, 1988 p329) The museum was built during Macedonian King Ptolemy A. Lagos's rule as a wing or addition to the Royal Macedonian Academy which was identical to the one in they had in Macedonia. The teachers, students and researchers working and studying at this institution were cared for by the state and their livelihood was supported by the King.

Agnes Savil's book "*Alexander the Great and his Time*" on p. 180 we find: "For a time Hellenism revived when Demetrius of Bactria, who was a half Macedonian and half Greek, tried in 187 B.C to reclaim the Indian empire of Alexander."

This statement clearly demonstrates that he was a Bactrian (modern day Afghanistan, Uzbekistan, and Tajikistan) that had one Macedonian parent (most probably his father as a father is always named first), and that his mother was from elsewhere which in ancient times could quite literally have been anywhere. Now, how do we deal with this quote according to the modern Greeks? Should we assume that there is such a person who is somehow both a half Greek and half Greek if Macedonians are supposedly Greeks all along?

This makes absolutely no sense.

Quintus Curtius Rufus wrote that during the fall in 330 B.C at the capital Drangien, later called Prodosi (due to the discovery of a plot against Alexander), Philotas was suspected of being a key participant in a plan for a rebellion and was put on trial for treason. The trial was public and conducted before an Assembly of the Macedonian Army which was the traditional way of conducting trials involving treason. During the trial, Alexander asked Philotas in a loud voice so that everyone could hear:

"Now the Macedonians will judge you, so I ask you will you reply in our native language." Philotas then said, "I prefer to speak in the Koine tongue which is the official language of the Macedonian Empire."
Alexander then responded by saying: "It is obvious that Philotas detests even our native language."
This was added to the reasons why Alexander executed him and evidence that his native tongue was **Macedonian**. The Macedonian language obviously existed.

The common tongue was called Koine, which was a language that was used for trade literally all over Europe, the Middle East, Africa, Egypt and from to Libya right up to Iberia (modern day Spain) over 2,000 years before a nation called Greece was ever created in 1830. Koine was the lingua franca of the time, much like how Latin was spoken and became the new lingua franca once Rome had conquered the world, as well as how it is now the English language which is spoken everywhere since the British Empire and all of their conquests.

The city-states had multiple languages and dialects, (none of which understood the Macedonian language), and it was the Koine language that was used for trade and state matters.
Greece adopted and instated this Koine language in 1832 when it was being formed as a country for the very first time in history, with Prince Otto of Bavaria (modern day Germany) as its head of state. Yes, you read that correct. Greece's first official King was a German.

Greece adopted and instated the Koine language as their national language in the 1830's because prior to this there was no such thing as a "Greek language". Koine as mentioned was just the ancient language of trade; so, are *all* these places on multiple continents *all* somehow "Greek" too now according to modern Greeks - who say that Alexander III was Greek because he was able to speak the 'Greek language'? No, of course not. It was the language that was used for trade everywhere! Much like Latin was and also how English is now used worldwide today which has nothing to do with Italy, Britain or The United Kingdom.

Not even the city-statesmen could understand one another with their multiple languages so it was Koine that was used between them for communication. Since 1830 the notion of anyone from the past speaking 'Greek' is by fact a false and incorrect sentence.

The city-statesmen spoke and used a variety of languages, among them being, Attic, Ionic, Aeolic, Arcadocypriot, Doric, Demotic, Pamphylian, Boiotic, Thessalic, Lesbic, Cypriot, Boeotian, Phocian (including Delphian), Locrian, Laconian, Heraclean, Messenian, Megarian, Corinthian, Argolic, Rhodian, Coan, Theran, Cyrenaean, Cretan, Sicilian, Elean, Dimotiki, Katharevousa, Pontic, Phanariot.
None of which were intelligible or understood by one another, hence Koine being the common language/tongue that was used between them when necessary and not used locally.
Now if they *were* in fact intelligible between themselves then you would have to ask yourself *why* would all of these documented languages have existed in the first place? This is why nobles and royalty from all corners of Europe, Asia and Africa could all speak and understand this same language, which has absolutely nothing to do with the modern state of Greece that adopted and formalised it 2,000 odd years later.

Are the ancient Africans, Egyptians, Persians, Spaniards, Nordics and Germanic people now somehow also Greeks? How absurd.

Quintus Rufus *"The History of Alexander"* "Accordingly, one festive day, Alexander had a sumptuous banquet organized so that he could invite not only his principal friends among the Macedonians and Greeks but also the enemy nobility." [p.188] Points of interest: 'Macedonians and Greeks'. If the ancient Macedonians were Greeks, then, only one identifier would have been sufficient. As you can see, the ancient authors clearly knew the difference between Macedonians and Greeks as being separate entities.

Quintus Rufus *"The History of Alexander"* At a banquet prepared by Alexander for the ambassadors of certain tribes from India, among the invited guests present was the Macedonian Horratas and the Greek boxer named Dioxippus. Now at the feast the Macedonian Horratas who was already drunk, began to make insulting comments to Dioxippus and to challenge him, if he were a man, to fight a duel. Dioxippus agreed and the two men fought rather a short fight with Dioxippus emerging a victor. A huge crowd of soldiers including the Greeks supported Dioxippus. "The outcome of the show dismayed Alexander, as well as the Macedonian soldiers, especially since the barbarians had been present, for he feared that a mockery had been made of the celebrated Macedonian valour." [p.229]

Point of interest: There are two fighters, one Macedonian, one Greek. A Macedonian had lost the fight and Alexander is dismayed. Why? How can a mockery be made of the Macedonian valour if in this fight the Greek won? If Alexander considered himself Greek, then, the outcome of the fight should have had no disturbing influence on him. But as we see he was dismayed. Peter Green says: "it was a matter of national prestige", and Bosworth states that the crowd was "ethnically polarized." This needs no further analysis. Ethnicity of the two fighters and their effect on the polarized crowd is not an option for consideration. It is a given.

Arrian *"The Campaigns of Alexander"* "Gentlemen of Macedon, and you my friends and allies, this must not be. Stand firm; for well you know that hardship and danger are the price of glory, and that sweet is the savour of a life of courage and of deathless renown beyond the grave." [p.294]

An obvious question: If Macedonians were Greeks, and if Macedonia was considered Greek land, then how can we reconcile with the fact that Alexander continually calls the Greeks "his allies" next to his Macedonians?

[Referring to Arrian's separation of Macedonians and Greeks] "The same painstaking attention to details is evident in administrative matters. Appointments of governors are duly mentioned, and throughout his book Arrian is careful to give the father's name in the case of Macedonians, e.g. Ptolemy son of Lagus, and in the case of Greeks it is only their city of origin." [p.25]

Arrian *"The Campaigns of Alexander"* "The backbone of the infantry was the Macedonian heavy infantry, the 'Foot Companions', organized on territorial basis in six battalions (taxeis) of about 1,500 men each. In place of the nine-foot spear carried by the Greek hoplite, the Macedonian infantryman was armed with a pike or sarissa about 13 to 14 feet long, which required both hands to wield it. The light circular shield was slung on the left shoulder and was smaller than that carried by the Greek hoplite which demanded the use of the left arm. Both, Greek and Macedonian infantry wore greaves and a helmet, but it is possible that the Macedonians did not wear a breastplate. The phalanx (a heavy infantry), like all the Macedonian troops

had been brought by Philip to a remarkable standard of training and discipline." [p.35]
Why would Arrian separate the two between Greeks and Macedonians?

Quintus Curtius Rufus "*The History of Alexander*" [The trial of Hermolaus]
"As for you Callisthenes, the only person to think you a man (because you are an assassin), I know why you want him brought forward. It is so that the insult which sometimes uttered against me and sometimes heard from him can be repeated by his lips before this gathering. Were he a Macedonian I would have introduced him here along with you - a teacher truly worth of his pupil. As it is, he is an Olynthian and does not enjoy the same rights." [p.195] [Since Callisthenes was a Greek Olynthian is clearly distinguished from that of the Macedonians.]

Robert A. Hudley in his paper "*Diodoros 18.60.1-3: "A Case of Remodelled Source Materials*" dissects "Eumenes"":
"We then come upon Eumenes' second observation that, being a foreigner, he has no right to exercise command over Macedonians. At no point, however, in Diodoros' prior narrative does Eumenes' Greek origin excite animosity among the Macedonians. More important, Eumenes does not see his foreign origin as an impediment to accepting the dynasty' offer of a supreme command in 18.58.4 and he proceeds to exercise that authority in 19.13.7 and 15.5 without any qualms on his part that he is not a Macedonian. Eumenes' foreign origin does become an issue at one point among the commanders of the Silver Shields."

Pierre Jouguet *"Alexander the Great and the Hellenistic World"*
Speaking of Eumenes:
"He knew from experience that in the eyes of the Macedonians he was still a Greek, a foreigner. Plutarch praised his charming and refined manners, which were very unlike the haughty airs of the noble Macedonian officer." [p.142]

More on Eumenes: "But he was not a Macedonian, and the Macedonians did not look upon him as an equal. This may have been one reason for his tenacious loyalty to the cause of the Kings; his fortune was bound up with the Empire, and in the case of a partition he would not have received the support of the Macedonian troops in securing a portion for himself." Ibid, [p.129]

On Isocrates: "At the end of his speech, Isocrates, summarizing the programme which he was proposing to Philip, advised him to be a benefactor to the Greeks, a King to his Macedonians, and to the barbarians not a master, but a chief." Ibid [p.106]

[On Macedonians and Greeks] "It is sufficient for our purposes to note that the Hellenes and the Macedonians regarded themselves as different nations, and this feeling did not cease to be the source of great difficulties for the union of Greece under Macedonian rule. When the union was achieved, it was only by policy of force." Ibid, [p.68]

Pierre Jouguet *"Alexander the Great and the Hellenistic World"*
"An Athenian decree, voted at his instigation [Chremonides] (266-265 or 265-264), declared an agreement between Athens and Sparta, always united against the enemies of the Hellenes" (Chremonidean War).
In this case, these "united Hellenes" were fighting against the Macedonian Antigonos. Here you have a clear delineation

between Hellenes [Athenians and Spartans] and their common enemy - the Macedonians. Why not accept the fate of the ancient authors and reconcile with the fact that ancient Macedonians were just that - Macedonians. There was nothing Hellenic about these loyal followers of their King and there was nothing Greek with these hardy warriors of Macedon. [p.187]

Wilcken's quotes from "*Alexander the Great*": On p.22-23. "Even in Philip's day the Greeks saw in the Macedonians a non-Greek foreign people and we must remember this if we are to understand the history of Philip and Alexander, and especially the resistance and obstacles which met them from the Greeks. The point is much more important than our modern conviction that Greeks and Macedonians were brethren, this was equally unknown to both and therefore could have no political effect."
On p.26: "The dislike was reciprocal, for the Macedonians have grown into a proud masterful nation, which with highly developed national consciousness looked down upon the Hellenes with contempt. This fact too is of prime importance for the understanding of later history."
On p.45 "The Greeks regarded the hegemony of Philip as after all, a foreign domination; they did not look upon the Macedonians as Greeks."

Lamian War 323-322 B.C is also known as the "Hellenic War" by its protagonists. The Greeks, the Hellenes, were fighting the Macedonians led by Antipater at Lamia.

During one of their campaigns south of Olympus, Macedonians took prisoners and Alexander asked one of the women who she was to which she replied: "I am the sister of Theogenes who commanded our army against your father Philip and fell at Chaeronea fighting for the liberty of Greece." If Philip and Alexander were Greeks themselves who were "unifying" the

Greek city states, then why were the so-called "Greeks" opposite Philip fighting for the liberty of Greece?

Weren't Thebans and Athenians and their allies fighting together for the holy soil of Hellas on August 2nd 338 B.C at the sleepy village of Chaeronea?

Fellow Hellenes being the Athenians and Thebans, fought *against* the Macedonians described as the barbarians from the north. If the Macedonians were "Greeks" then this would have been a civil war. If Macedonians were Greeks, why did they not fight together to safeguard "the holy soil of Hellas" for the "liberty of Greece from outsiders" instead of against one another?

Lycurgus quoted as stating: [after the battle of Chaeronea] "With the death was buried the freedom of Greece."

Polybius *"The Rise of the Roman Empire"* Polybius reports on the speech made by Agelaus of Naupactus at the first conference in the presence of the King and the allies. He spoke as follows: [A selected segment from his speech] "I therefore beg you all to be on your guard against this danger, and I appeal especially to King Philip. [Philip V] For you the safest policy, instead of wearing down the Greeks and making them an easy prey for the invader, is to take care of them as you would of your own body, and to protect every province of Greece as you would if it were a part of your own dominions. If you follow this policy, the Greeks will be your friends and your faithful allies in case of attack, and foreigners will be the less inclined to plot against your throne, because they will be discouraged by the loyalty of the Greeks towards you." [p 45]

Polybius *"The Rise of the Roman Empire"* "instead of wearing down the Greeks" "making them an easy prey for the invader" "to protect every province of Greece as you would if it were a part of your own dominions". Polybius clearly distinguished not only between Greeks and Macedonians in the above passage, but also between the lands of Greece and Macedonia. [p .300.] (book 5.104)

F.W. Wallbank *"The Hellenistic World"* [p 49] "While Craterus and Antipater collaborated under the command of the latter to suppress a Greek revolt (the so-called Lamian War ended in a crushing blow to the Greeks and especially Athens), Perdiccas took control of the kings."

Points of interest: "ended in a crushing blow to the Greeks and especially Athens". Very clearly the Lamian war ended with a victory of the Macedonians over the Greeks (Athenians being part of that Greek force).

When another Macedonian king, Archelaus (413 to 399 B.C) attacked Larissa in Thessaly, Thrasymachus wrote what was to later become a "model oration" on behalf of the Larissans. Only one sentence has survived which reads as follows: "Shall we be slaves to Archelaus, we, being Greeks, to a barbarian?"

If the ancient Macedonians were Greek, then why did Thrasymachus refer to them not only as barbarians but very much distinguished them from "Greeks"?

Here there is a relative abundance of information from Arrian, Plutarch (Alexander, Eumenes), Diodorus 17-20, Justin, Curtius Rufus, and Nepos (Eumenes), based upon Greek and Greek-derived Latin sources. It is clear that over a five-century span of writing in multiple languages, representing a variety of historiographical and philosophical positions the ancient writers regarded the Greeks and the Macedonians as two separate and distinct peoples whose relationship was marked by "considerable antipathy, if not outright hostility."

The conclusion is still the same - the Ancient Macedonians were not Greeks. If they were, they would have been called Greeks, not Macedonians, and they would not have been specifically distinguished from the Greeks by ancient authors including the ancient Greek authors themselves. Nothing could be further from the truth than to claim that the ancient Macedonians and the ancient Greeks were brethren. They were simply two different people.

What about Demosthenes and what he had to say about the Macedonians, particularly about Philip II? Modern day Greeks would like to dispatch off Demosthenes' castigations of Philip II as political rhetoric, and yet Demosthenes was twice appointed to lead the war effort of Athens against Macedonia. He, Demosthenes, said of Philip that "Philip was not Greek, nor related to Greeks but comes from Macedonia where a person could not even buy a decent slave". Soon after his death the people of Athens paid him fitting honours by erecting his statue made of bronze. On the base of his statue the following famous inscription was carved: "If only your strength had been equal, Demosthenes, to your wisdom, never would Greece have been ruled by a Macedonian Ares".

The actions of his contemporaries, the ancient "Greeks" speak much louder about Demosthenes' character than the words of any modern Greek. Demosthenes, in modern terms was a patriot, not a crackpot politician and they even erected a bronze statue of him! The speech from his third Philippic had success and Demosthenes was awarded with a golden wreath.

Another war started in Boeotia. Athens and Thebes had won twice during the battles at Parapotamii so that Philip did not manage to break through Boeotia. This success increased the popularity of Demosthenes, who brought a decision in the Macedonian Assembly to declare a war against Philip. As an award, Demosthenes once again was crowned with a golden wreath for his political activities in favour of the state.

When news of Philip's death reached Athens, Demosthenes appeared in public dressed in magnificent attire and wore a garland on his head. The following is what was subsequently written about that moment in history: "For my part I cannot say that the Athenians did themselves any credit in putting on garlands and offering sacrifices to celebrate the death of a king who, when he was the conqueror and they the conquered had treated them with such tolerance and humanity. Far apart from provoking the anger of the gods, it was a contemptible action to make Philip a citizen of Athens and pay him honours while he was alive, and then, as soon as he has fallen by another's hand, to be besides themselves with joy, trample on his body and sing paeans of victory, as though they themselves have accomplished some great feat of arms."

If the Macedonians were Greek, then why did so many Greeks join the ranks of the Persians to fight against the Macedonians? Weren't the Persians the supposed worst enemies of the Greeks? If Alexander indeed fought the Persians to avenge the "Greeks" shouldn't the Greeks have willingly and voluntarily joined him? "Darius' Greeks fought to thrust the Macedonians back into the water and save the day for their left wing, already in retreat, while the Macedonians, in their turn, with Alexander's triumph plain before their eyes, were determined to equal his success and not forfeit the proud title of invincible, hitherto universally bestowed upon them. The fight was further embittered by the old racial rivalry of Greek and Macedonian."

For those that suggest that Philip II "unified" the ancient city states or the "Greeks" into the fold with Macedonians as being one and the same, then please read the next quote very carefully. "Alexander meanwhile dealt swiftly with the unrest in Greece - not only did the Athenians rejoice at Philip's death, but the Aetolians, the Thebans, as well as the Spartans and the Peloponnesians, were ready to throw off the Macedonian yoke".

If you read the quote carefully you would have noticed the word "yoke". The Aetolians, Thebans, Spartans, and Peloponnesians were ready to throw off the 'Macedonian yoke'. Allow me to emphasize that, when one "unifies" there is no "yoke" to be thrown off.
"Alexander also referred to his father Philip as conqueror of Athenians and recalled to their minds the recent conquest of Boeotia and the annihilation of its best-known city." Allow me to once again emphasize that when one "unifies" there is no "conquest" to be had.

What is not abundantly clear here? Need anyone say any more?

Apparently with some, there is such a need so here are some more quotes by Quintus Rufus *"The History of Alexander"*: "Men! If you consider the scale of our achievements, your longing for peace and your weariness of brilliant campaigns are not at all surprising. Let me pass over the Illyrians, the Triballians, Boeotia, Thrace, Sparta, the Achaeans, the Peloponnesians - all of them subdued under my direct leadership or by campaigns conducted under my orders of instructions".

(When one "unites", one does not "subdue" or "force submission" or "conquer" people). "Starting with Macedonia, I now have power over Greece; I have brought Thrace and the Illyrians under my control; rule the Triballi and the Maedi. I have Asia in my possession from the Hellespont to the Red Sea."

According to Arrian in *"The Campaigns of Alexander"*, Alexander continues to speak to his Macedonians and allies: "Come, then; add the rest of Asia to what you already possess - a small addition to the great sum of your conquests. What great or noble work could we ourselves have achieved had we thought it enough living at ease in Macedon, merely to guard our homes, excepting no burden beyond checking the encroachment of the Thracians on our borders, or the Illyrians and Triballians, or perhaps such Greeks as might prove a menace to our comfort."

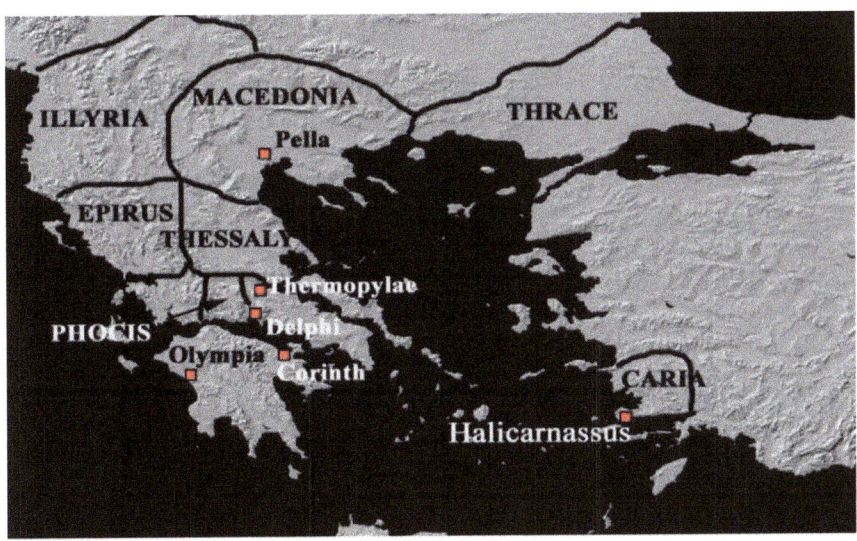

MACEDONIA
Mount Olympus
AEGEAN SEA
IONIA
Thermopylae
Thebes
Marathon
Corinth
Athens
Olympia
Salamis
Sparta
MEDITERRANEAN SEA
CRETE

MACEDONIA
THRACE
Philippi
Thessalonica
Beroea
Troas
ACHAIA
AEGEAN SEA
ASIA
Corinth
Athens
Ephesus
CRETE

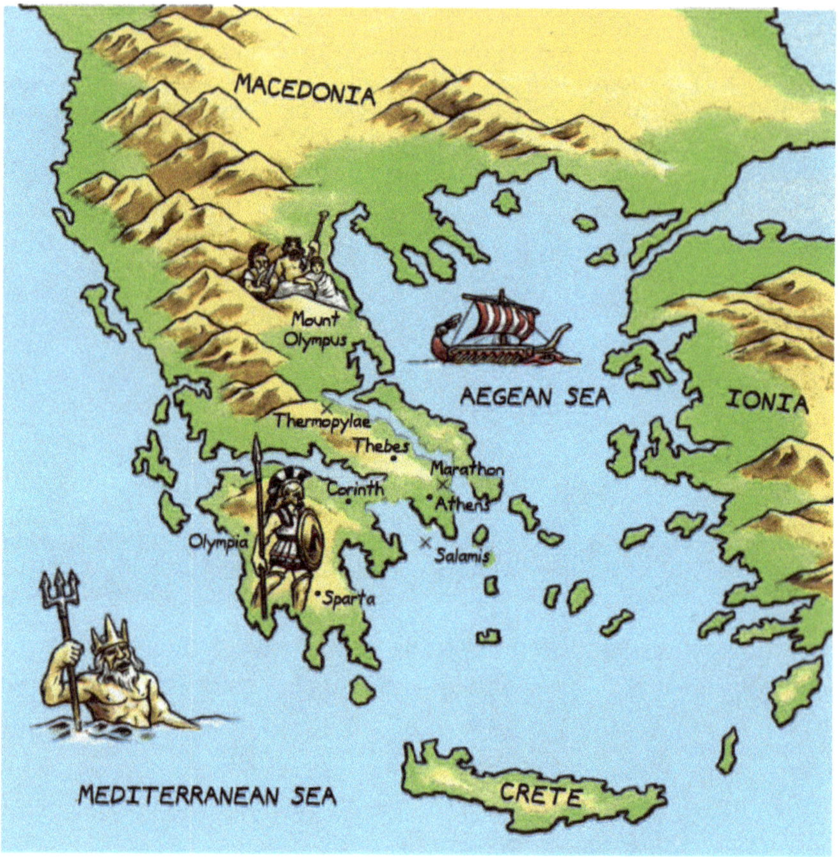

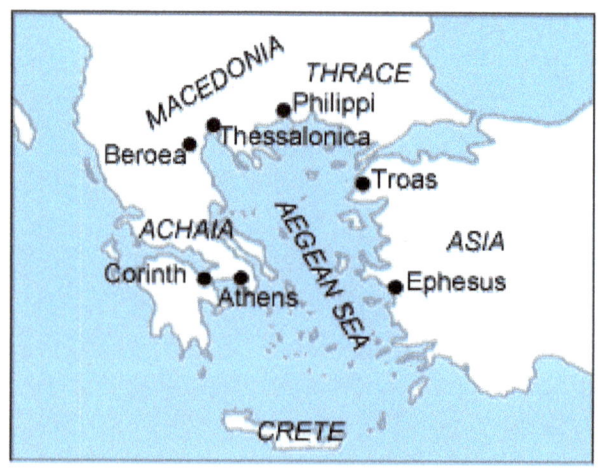

It is well documented that the first Macedonian-Roman War (215-205 B.C), then the second Macedonian-Roman war (200-197 B.C) was a failure for King Philip V and the Macedonian state. In this war the Romans were attacking together with the armies of the Illyrians, Dardanians and some of the city-states, among of which were Athens, Rhodes and Pergam.

Why would democratic city-states join the fight against a monarchist kingdom of Macedonia if they were indeed of the same people?

Perseus (179–168 B.C) – the last Macedonian King of the Antigonid Dynasty.
This ruler continued implementing the policy of his father, secured the northern boundaries of Macedonia, campaigned against Thracians, renewed the treaty with Rome in order to be acclaimed the King of Macedonia and led the third Macedonian-Roman war. After long preparations, Rome declared war to Macedonia (171 B.C). The 13,000 numbered Roman army landed in Illyria and started helping the Hellenic city-states. Perseus, at the Macedonian Assembly brought a decision to initiate the war. He gathered 14,000 soldiers in his army and enormous war reserves for a 10-year war period. During the first year of the war Perseus blocked all crossings from Thessaly to Macedonia and disabled the pervasion of the Roman Army.

Macedonia being the largest and most powerful monarchy-led country in the region (something that *neither* of the neighbouring states were or had), was the very last to fall under Roman rule. Lesser democratic city-states were taken over rather quickly. With the decision of the Roman Senate in 148 B.C, Macedonia was transformed into a Roman province. The establishment of the direct Roman administrative system with the permanent provincial governor with the capital in

Thessalonica (Solun) was followed by the allocation of permanent Roman garrisons.

Much like the garrisons that were installed by Alexander III all over the city-states when he embarked to go on his Asian campaign, Rome installed them in Macedonia. Garrisons are *only ever* installed in conquered territories by foreigners, hence, why the Macedonians were viewed as foreigners and vice versa by the city-states.

Under the Roman Empire (with Macedonia being the last to fall to Roman rule), Macedonia was eventually divided up into Macedonia prima and Macedonia secunda (or salutaris) to try to reduce its power.

By the direct involvement of the Goths headed by Alaric, the Byzantine imperial court managed to secure the control over this controversial part of the Balkans. Inciting Alaric's campaign in Italy in 401, Byzantium successfully liberated itself from the presence of the Goths. The same year the Byzantine imperial court under Justinian I (who was himself a Macedonian, born in Macedonia near the city of Skopje) abolished the province of *Macedonia Salutaris* and reestablished a sole province of Macedonia.

It is interesting to note here before I continue, that the Macedonian word for King is Czar/Tsar/Tzar.

As it was Macedonia that was the ruling empire of the time ***prior*** to the fall to Rome, it is also interesting that the Romans chose to name all their emperors "Caesar" thereafter, which is the Latinized version of the word Czar/Tsar/Tzar.

Latin like all the romantic languages, often place the letter C in place for the "ts" sound as we have in Czar/Tsar/Tzar, so therefore, Czar/Tsar/Tzar becomes C-Zar (ts-zar) which is where we get the word "Caesar" from in English or "Ce'zar".

The Koine/modern Greek word for King is "Vasilias" which is not even close.

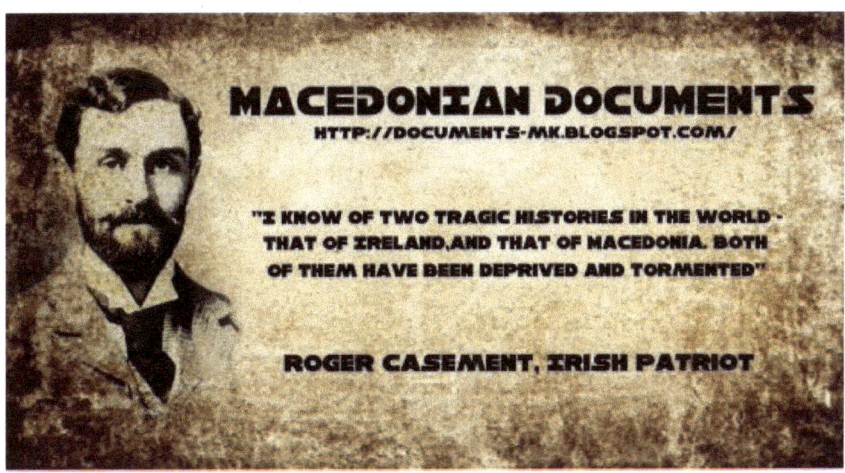

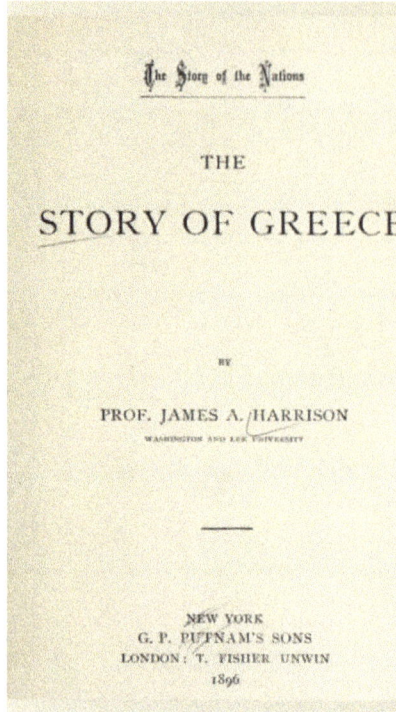

THE RISE OF THEBES.   477

Some of the cities were even garrisoned by Spartan troops.

Two most noble figures appear on the stage of Grecian history just at this point, men in whose veins Theban blood coursed richly, men who forever lift Thebes out of the reproach of insignificance and unproductiveness, and place her worthily alongside of Athens and Sparta as a motherland of great men. Our triangle of Grecian story has these three illuminated points—ATHENS, SPARTA, THEBES—each pointing in a different direction, each the result of differing historical conditions, each haply the product of climate and circumstance; all Greek at the core, and all illustrating in multifarious ways the fertile genius of the Greek race. The Macedonians were not Greeks.

As we have given so much attention to Athens and Lacedæmon in the course of our tale, let us now turn for a little moment to this third great exponent of Hellenic ideas and gifts, THEBES, and see if we cannot extract from her too, in the persons of her great men, something individual and characteristic.

Epaminondas and Pelopidas were both Thebans, and were united by one of the most beautiful friendships known in history. The one—Pelopidas—shone forth no less amid his riches than the other—Epaminondas—loomed forth from the midst of his poverty. They were both born of honorable race. Others permitted themselves to be obliged by Pelopidas, and thankfully made use of his liberality and kindness; but amongst all his friends he never could persuade Epaminondas to be a sharer of his wealth. Being

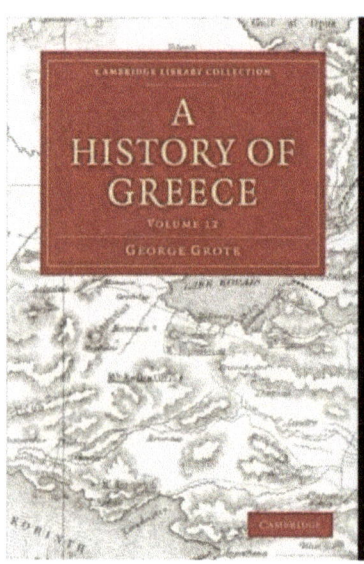

Alexander (born in July 356 B.C.), like his father Philip, was not a Greek, but a Macedonian and Epirot, partially imbued with Grecian sentiment and intelligence. It is true that his ancestors, some centuries before, had been emigrants from Argos; but the kings of Macedonia had long lost all trace of any such peculiarity as might originally have distinguished them from their subjects. The basis of Philip's character was Macedonian, not Greek: it was the self-will of a barbarian prince, not the *ingenium civile*, or sense of reciprocal obligation

Macedonia: A History

NONSENSICAL MIGRATION THEORY WHICH HAS NEVER BEEN PROVEN AND REJECTED AS FACT

There simply was no mass colonisation of "Slavs invading" or "taking over" anywhere in the 6th century as has often been suggested. The only source for this absurdity exists on Wikipedia – a website that any 8-year-old with a keyboard can change and edit to whatever they want it to say. "The sky is brown, and oceans are actually pink! Pigs do indeed fly and elephants fit in your fridge". Sure, it says so right there on Wikipedia! they say as though Wikipedia is any possible form of factually based information.

This has only ever been a theory pushed forward (possibly even invented by) which the Greek state considers and treats as fact to assist in their cause when no such study has *ever* proven that this *ever* took place.

Even if it *were* true! How on Earth could peaceful nomadic people allegedly invade or take over anywhere; when according to their own theory they were identified only as farmers, and not once ever mentioned as being a warrior type people of any sort? So, did a collection of farmer families now somehow displace the entire population, beliefs, language, culture etc. of an entire country?

One country that they state now has never even existed mind you.

Now add to this, there were no such things as physical borders, border security or border patrol checkpoints between nations or countries anywhere for that matter, which has only ever existed within the last 100 years or so. So, what now then? Did this group of farmers according to their own theory somehow know or understand to stop at this imaginary, unseen and non-existent border not entering the region of Greece at all?
Because remember, "they're all Slavs" and it's the Greeks that are stating that they are a 100% homogenous nation related to the ancient Greeks, that are 98% Christian Greeks and 2% Muslim Greeks, and that there are only Greeks living in Greece!

You honestly couldn't even make this stuff up if you tried. This is literally according to the current Greek government and census data.

When Alexander conquered and subdued Eastern Europe on his path during his conquests of Asia, he created cities and populated them (as well as in the existing cities) with his Macedonians. These people were from the injured soldiers or those that were getting too old to continue fighting. Soldiers that met and married the local women. These cities remained intact and vibrant even after the Macedonian empire had long ended.

History has also recorded that when Rome finally attacked Macedonia, that half of the Macedonian population fled as far north and east as possible beyond the reach of Roman domain. The people that fled were mostly educated and prominent Macedonians not equipped with the skills to fight and who also would have found it difficult to survive under Roman oppression. They were invariably civilized and capable of spreading the Macedonian language and culture to the new lands that they had settled in.

Remember, that it was Macedonia prior to the Roman conquests were the ruling empire of Europe at the time. It is estimated that half a million people fled from Macedonia some 2,000 years ago and since then had been populating and spreading the Macedonian culture and language within Eastern Europe and northwest Asia all the way out to Siberia.

When these so-called "Slav tribes" from north of the Danube all the way out to Siberia were Christianised during the 8th, 9th and 10th centuries AD, they were Christianised by the teachers from Macedonia (teachers at the time were simply the church leaders), which to them was apparently a foreign world, a world that should have been alien and unfamiliar to these "Slavs".
Yet somehow and for some reason, this constant demand for Macedonian teachers *did* in fact happen and lead to the formation of the Ohrid University, which has been established was to become the very first University in all of Europe!
"The reason that these people were asking for teachers from Macedonia" explains Markus "is because they either *were* themselves or believed to be themselves akin to the Macedonians".
This could also explain why when these so-called "Slavs" came to Macedonia (if it indeed happened) as they had found a familiar culture and language based on their own ancestry.

It is noted that Alexander III, his father Philip II and many other Macedonian kings even prior to them never implemented the death sentence that was imposed for crimes committed by citizens of Macedonia (except in the cases of treason), and that the sentence for serious crimes was indefinite exile for the criminal as well as their entire families which was used as a deterrent for such crimes, to as far away as they possibly knew to the region of Scythia - which as it turns out also happens to be the region of the modern day country of Ukraine.

Ukraine in English (or U-kraj, kraj) in the Macedonian language means "the end", as it was the end of the known world for the people of the time.
Slav/Slava in the Macedonian language means a celebration, so after Roman rule had ended in the 5th Century; these could possibly have just been the exiled criminal native Macedonians families returning to their ancestral homeland many centuries later - as all the rulers both domestic and foreign were finally gone after the collapse of the Roman Empire.

If Macedonians are as our neighbours would love to say "Slavs that invaded in the 6th century" (which we have already outlined that obviously didn't happen), we note that it's quite interesting that it was only in the 9th century (some 300 years later), that the Macedonian brothers Cyril and Methodius (Kiril I Metodija) who were both born in Solun (Thessalonica) which came from very respected families, and that these same teachers, these same church leaders and brothers, created the "new" Macedonian alphabet that was based on the language of the Macedonians, a language from the very same country that they were born in, so Solun (Thessalonica) is clearly in no logical way shape or form "Greek".

You won't find people in China becoming famous and celebrated for over 1,000 years for teaching the locals from China to read and write in Spanish now, would you?
That would make no sense at all because it's simply not the language that they speak there!

There are slight variants of this very same Macedonic language and alphabet that is used extensively throughout Eastern Europe back then as much as it is today. The modern Greeks are quite happy to say that they (the brothers) were Greeks, but these Macedonian brothers didn't spend decades forming and

teaching an alphabet, or using a language that the modern Greeks currently do (already established as being Koine), and then going out and spreading this very same language and alphabet all over Eastern Europe now did they?
No, it was Macedonian, because they *were* Macedonian and *spoke* Macedonian.
They'll say that these Slavs invaded Macedonia – yet somehow, it's the same Macedonian language and alphabet that is used and was then spread to those foreign lands 200-300 centuries earlier.

Then from our other neighbour, there's that equally nonsensical claim that the brothers were Bulgarian - not limited to the fact that there was no such thing as a "Bulgaria" in the 6th century, as it was only first created in 1870 and known as Thrace prior to that as well as the fact that they were born in Solun (Salonika/Thessalonica).

So, which is it then? They can't be Greeks as they didn't study, invent, teach or spread the Koine language over an area thousands of kilometres wide so what possible sense would that make?

They can't be Bulgarians if they were born in Solun (Salonika/Thessalonica), as Bulgaria didn't even exist at the time so how can they be? (modern day Bulgarian land is *always* cited as being Thrace prior to 1870).

The fact remains that they spoke, taught, spread, lived, and breathed Macedonian so there's everyone's answer. Occam's razor - the most likely solution is usually the simplest one.
They were Macedonian pure and simple. Born in Solun Macedonia.

Studied under Clement and Naum at the very first University in Europe at Ohrid, Macedonia.
They spoke and taught the language of the people, the Macedonians in Macedonia.

How could this possibly be even up for any debate?

They were recognised as Macedonians back in the 9th Century, and impossibly enough even gaining permission and allowed by the Holy See (after hundreds of years of Roman rule where Catholicism and Latin was *still* the lingua franca of the time), to conduct Holy Liturgy services <u>*in Rome*</u> mind you, in the Macedonian language way back in 867. This is documented as fact.

So much for "the Macedonian language doesn't exist; Macedonia doesn't exist; you are an invention of Tito in 1945".

It was directly reflected in Macedonia where the legacy of the Kiril and Metodija's (Cyril and Methodius) literary and linguistic work was incorporated into the activity of their most prominent disciples Clement and Naum, who during the last decades of the 9th century and the beginning of the 10th century, developed comprehensive spiritual, cultural and educational activity in their native country of Macedonia, at the very first University in Europe.
They revised the Glagolic script which received its name from the Macedonian word "glagol" which in English means "word" and the word "glagolati" meaning "to speak".
For those at the time who had never even seen a book in their life before, it appeared as though the letters spoke to the reader and told him what to say. This is the very same Cyrillic script in the Macedonian language as well as its variations that is used all over Eastern Europe today.

The Macedonian language is *not* fully intelligible with the Bulgarian language as Bulgarians like to suggest. There are some similar words here or there perhaps, but that's the exact same thing as with Russian, Slovak, Czech, Polish, Serbian, Croatian, Slovenian etc. as it is used all over Eastern Europe.

That is because the root language for them all is Macedonian, and not the other way around.

The nonsensical claims of Macedonia's neighbouring countries have their constantly changing stories a little backwards (actually, *very* backwards) - and then think it's normal to continue to change their story when and how they see fit to suit whatever narrative it is they are trying to suggest at the time - which *still* doesn't make any logical sense according to literally all history that has been documented and published anywhere at all on this subject.

We don't speak a variant of *their* language – they speak a variant of *ours*.

Macedonia: A History

INDO-EUROPEAN LANGUAGES

BRANCH	GROUP	LANGUAGES AND MAJOR DIALECTS			PROVENIENCE
		ANCIENT	MEDIEVAL	MODERN	
GERMANIC	East	Gothic			eastern Europe
	North		Old Norse	Icelandic	Iceland
				Faroese	Faroe islands
				Norwegian	Norway
				Swedish	Sweden
				Danish	Denmark
	West		Old High German	German	Germany, Switzerland, Austria
			Middle High German		
			Old Saxon	Yiddish	Germany, eastern Europe
			Middle Low German	Low German	Northern Germany
			Middle Dutch	Dutch	Netherlands
				Afrikaans	So. Africa
			Middle Flemish	Flemish	Belgium
			Old Frisian	Frisian	Netherlands, Germany
			Old English	English	England
			Middle English		
CELTIC	Continental	Goulish			Gaul
	Brythonic		Old Welsh	Welsh	Wales
			Middle Welsh		
			Old Cornish	Cornish	Cornwall
			Middle Breton	Breton	Brittany
	Goidelic		Old Irish	Irish Gaelic	Ireland
			Middle Irish		
				Scottish Gaelic	Scotland
				Manx	Isle of Man
ITALIC	Osco-Umbrian	Oscan, Sabellian, Umbrian			ancient Italy
	Latinian or Romance	Venetic, Faliscan, Lanuvian, Praenestine, Latin			ancient Italy
				Portuguese	Portugal
				Spanish	Spain
				Judeo-Spanish	Mediterranean lands
				Catalan	Spain (Catalonia)
			Old Provençal	Provençal	southern France
			Old French	French	France, Belgium, Switzerland
			Middle French		
				Haitian Creole	Haiti
				Italian	Italy, Switzerland
				Rhaeto-Romanic	Switzerland, Italy
				Sardinian	Sardinia
				Dalmatian	Adriatic coast
				Romanian	Romania, Balkans
Scantily recorded and of uncertain affinities within Indo-European		Ligurian, Messapian, Phrygian			ancient Italy, Asia Minor
Albanian				Albanian	Albania, southern Italy
Greek		Greek	Greek	Greek	Greece, the eastern Mediterranean
Baltic			Old Prussian		East Prussia
				Lithuanian	Lithuania
				Latvian	Latvia
MACEDONIC	South	Macedonian	Macedonian	Macedonian	Macedonia
				Slovene	Yugoslavia
				Serbo-Croatian	Yugoslavia
				Bulgarian	Bulgaria
	West			Czech, Slovak	Czechoslovakia
				Polish, Kashubian	Poland
				Wendish, Polabian	Germany
	East			Russian	Russia
				Ukrainian	Ukraine
				Belorussian	White Russia
Armenian		Armenian	Armenian	Armenian	Asia Minor, Caucasus
IRANIAN	West	Old Persian	Pahlavi		Persia
			Persian	Persian	Persia (Iran)
				Kurdish	Persia, Iraq, Turkey
				Baluchi	West Pakistan
				Tajiki	central Asia
	East	Avestan			ancient Persia
			Sogdian		central Asia
			Khotanese		central Asia
				Pashto	Afghanistan, West Pakistan
				Ossetic	Caucasus
	Dard			Shina, Khowar, Kafiri	upper Indus valley
				Kashmiri	Kashmir
INDIC	Sanskritic	Sanskrit, Pali, Prakrits	Prakrits		India
				Lahnda	western Punjab
				Sindhi	Sind
				Panjabi	Punjab
				Rajasthani	Rajasthan
				Gujarati	Gujarat
				Marathi	western India
				Konkani	western India
				Oriya	Orissa
				Bengali	Bengal
				Assamese	Assam
				Bihari	Bihar
				Hindi	northern India
				Urdu	Pakistan, India
				Nepali	Nepal
				Sinhalese	Ceylon
				Romany	uncertain
Tocharian			Tocharian A, Tocharian B		central Asia

The following is sometimes considered as another branch of Indo-European, and sometimes as coordinate with Indo-European, the two together constituting Indo-Hittite.

| Anatolian | | Hittite, Lydian, Lycian, Luwian, Palaic, Hieroglyphic Hittite | | | ancient Asia Minor |

[1] Italics denote dead languages. Listing of a language only in the ancient or medieval columns but in roman type indicates that it survives only in some special use, as in literary composition or liturgy.
[2] Romance is normally applied only to medieval and modern languages; Latinian is normally applied only to ancient languages.

Simon Tasievski

MACEDONIA DURING BYZANTIAN RULE

Besides the immense Macedonian contribution to the arts, crafts, literature and architecture, Macedonians also served the Byzantine Empire as soldiers, statesmen and even as Emperors. Macedonians occupied the Empire's throne during the period from 867 AD to 1081 AD in what came to be known as the Macedonian Epoch.

The following Macedonian Emperors and Empresses served on the Byzantine throne: Basil I the Macedonian (867-886), Leo VI the Philosopher or the Wise (886-912), Alexander (886-913), Constantine VII Porphyrogenitus (913-959) alongside Romanus I Lecapenus (919-944), Romanus II (959-963), Nicephorus II Phocas (963-969), John Tzimisces (969-976), Basil II the Macedonian (976-1025), Constantine VIII (1025-1028), Romanus III Argyrus (1028-1034), Michael IV (1034-1041), Michael V Calaphates (1041-1042), Zoe and Theodora 1042, Constantine IX Monomachus (1042-1055) and Theodora (1055-1056). A. Vasiliev. *"History of the Byzantine Empire (324 - 1453)"*. The University of Wisconsin Press. 1952. (Pages 300-303).

Further proof of the brothers Kiril and Metodija (Cyril and Methodius) teachings and spread of Macedonian culture and language throughout the Byzantine Empire.

According to Byzantine sources, Nikola the father, along with his four sons being the brothers David, Moses, Aaron and Samoil belonged to a class of prominent and powerful dignitaries called Bolyars who were very influential in court. The brothers decided to rule their newly established state jointly. Unfortunately, the joint rule did not last long as three of the brothers died one after another leaving Samoil as the sole heir of the new state.

Samoil formed a state in the heartland of Macedonia and later turned it into a vast empire that rivalled that of Philip II. Initially Samoil raised his army from the Macedonian population and by the end of the 10th century he had conquered (in modern state terms) the southern half of Bulgaria, Serbia, Croatia, Albania, and most of the Greek territory. He created a large Macedonian state, which extended from the Black Sea to the Adriatic Sea, and from the Sava River to the Ionian Sea.

Samoil proclaimed himself Czar/Tzar (Emperor) and was even crowned by the Roman Pope.
His first Capital was at Prespa, and then Ohrid, both of which are in Macedonia. Ohrid also became the centre of the Macedonian Ohrid Archbishopric.

What fuelled the creation of such a nation was the Macedonian people who at the time found themselves exploited by all sides; and sought their struggle for independence through the rebellion lead by the Komitopuli brothers and then by Samoil and his successors.

The war between the Byzantines and the Macedonians lasted for 48 years from 970 to 1018 during which time thirteen major battles and several minor ones were fought. Samoil's military, political, and strategic mission was to create a strong and independent Macedonian state. He started accomplishing that mission immediately after Byzantium had conquered the eastern parts of Thrace (what is now Bulgaria). The territory on which Samoil established the medieval Macedonian state was almost the same size as the state of the previous Macedonian King Philip II, which infuriated Basil II who initiated the first campaign in 995 against Samoil. It was by no accident that Samoil received his strongest support from the Macedonian heartland defined by the triangle of the Vardar River, Ohrid and Mt. Shar. Samoil's success was fuelled by the Bogomil movement and its distaste for foreign rule. In Macedonia, the Bogomil movement was particularly influential in the creation of favourable conditions for a liberation uprising and the formation of an independent state. Samoil took full advantage of the situation and reestablished the Macedonian state. Samoil's kingdom had completely different domestic and foreign policies than his neighbours with several Capitals including Prespa, Ohrid, Prilep, Bitola, Pronishte and Setin which he alternatively used from time to time, all of which are located inside the heartland of Macedonia.

The famous and historic Archbishopric of Ohrid was created during Samoil's reign. Initially the Archbishopric was seated in Prespa, but when Samoil moved to Ohrid he brought it with him. Ohrid became his Capital as well as his religious centre. After its consolidation, the new Archbishop was given authority over all bishops who fell under Samoil's jurisdiction.

Unfortunately, the Byzantines also as Orthodox Christians refused to recognize the Archbishop of Ohrid, probably because the Roman Church which crowned Samoil had consecrated it, even though he himself was an Orthodox Christian.

During Samoil's rule the Macedonian Church was quite popular and the clergy, especially the bishops, enjoyed their privileged positions. These were the teachers and church leaders throughout the empire.

By August 1018, Basil II succeeded in destroying the last remnants of Samoil's forty-two-year reign (976-1018) of his

Macedonian kingdom. Once Basil II conquered Macedonia, he made it into a Byzantine province and sub-divided it into themes - once again to quell it's dominant power. He then installed a large army and garrisons to try to keep the peace.

Once again, evidence that garrisons are only used by an invading and foreign force and even though Basil II was a Macedonian by nationality and heritage, he viewed himself as a Byzantine first and we all know there is no such country as Byzantia.

IMPORTANT REFERENCES

The term 'Hellenism' was first introduced in historiography by German historian Droysen in 1877/78, in his publication *"Geschiehte des Hellenismus, I-III, Gotha"*. Johann Gustav Droysen was a consultant to the Bavarian Prince Otto at his coronation in May 1832, when he was crowned King Othonos I (Othönos A'), king of Greece, right after Greece gained its independence from the Ottoman Empire.

This was when the Greeks formed a consolidated Hellenic state for the first time in history. The regions consolidated under the first Hellada included the Peloponnesus, the Cyclades Islands, and the mainland from the Gulf of Arta to the west to the Gulf of Volos to the north. Greece's first Capital was a city called Naphplion located in Argolis Bay on the Peloponnesus seaside and *not* at Athens. Note that the Gulf of Volos is not even remotely close to Mount Olympus let alone its current border with Macedonia.

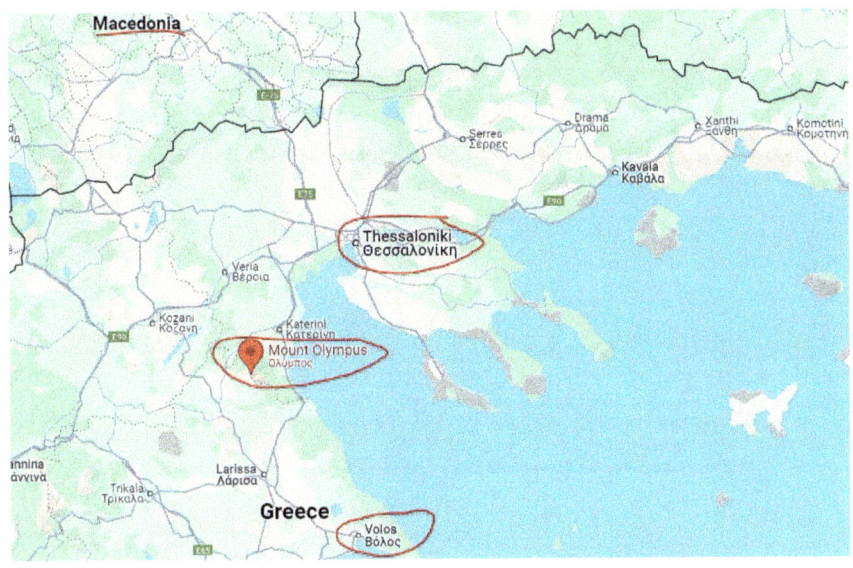

The moment the new state appeared, it immediately formed plans to enlarge itself giving birth to the "Megale Idea", which basically became a dominant idea for attempting to restore the Byzantine Empire. The "Megale Idea", which basically meant "Megale Hellada" (Greater Greece), was the axiom and foreign policy of the new monarchy. Under the term "helenismòs", the Greek monarchy attempted to conquer the physical territory stretching from Chemosh (Balkan Mountains) to Tenar on the Adriatic, to the Black Sea and to Mount Tauro in Asia Minor. (Svorönos, 1976, 81).

The Austrian, Carl Hron in his book *"The nationality of the Macedonians"* (1890) would underline: "Through my own studies, I came to the conclusion that Macedonians, are a separate nation by its history as well as by its own language".

The Carnegie Report in 1913 outlines the atrocities committed during the Balkan Wars by the Serbians, Greeks and Bulgarians against the Macedonians in the country of Macedonia.

How is it even possible that one family; all living together in the same household and under the same roof, 3 siblings by birth and all born in the same place were classed as either Serbs, Greeks or Bulgarians which was decided on which school or church they attended as often siblings attended different schools according to their age. It was the 3 neighbouring countries forcing the Macedonian population into submission by tearing apart the country depending on their own individual aspirations through the use of terror tactics.

Would someone care to explain how I have personally found well over 80 articles from various news publications and organisations, from all around the world dated between 1814 and 1947 that all refer to Macedonia as being a completely different entity to that of Serbia, Greece or Bulgaria, and all reporting on the atrocities committed against the Macedonian people by these same Serbs, Greeks and Bulgarians? (see chapter on Newspaper articles)

Press and Sun-Bulletin
20 Jan 1908, Mon · Page 1

MANY MACEDONIANS KILLED BY GREEKS

Sofia, Bulgaria, Jan. 20.—News has reached here of a terrible tragedy at Dragosh, Macedonia, several days ago. While a festival was in progress and the villagers were dancing upon the lawns in the public park, a large band of Greeks suddenly swooped down upon them and after driving them into their houses set fire to the buildings and burned them to death. The victims included women and children, and numbered, it is said, between 25 and 45.

Iakovakis Rizos Nerulos, president of the Athens Archaeological Society in his speech at the Acropolis on May 12th, 1841, said: "Philip not only defeated Greece at Chaeronea but he did something deadlier than that, he installed Alexander." (Lithoksoou, D., Symmiktos Laos, Mpatavia, Thessaloniki, 2005; Translation: Az-Buki, Skopje, 2005.)

During the Balkan wars in the early 1900's, every neighbour of Macedonia had already been liberated from the Ottoman yoke, and it was only Macedonia, the one that historically always had the most power that remained firmly in its grasp. Once the Ottomans were finally pushed out it quickly became a scavenger hunt by these neighbouring countries to rip apart and take pieces of it for themselves.

This is why the Treaty of Bucharest in 1913 was implemented, which prove the <u>undeniable fact</u> that Macedonia in that year was indeed partitioned amongst its neighbouring countries.
Being that it was *partitioned*, then we have ourselves undeniable proof that none of the new invaders and neighbouring countries had ever 'owned' that land to begin with as they claim.

Goce Delcev, Yane Sandanski, and Dame Gruev amongst many others were all Macedonians whose motto during the Balkan Wars was "Macedonia for the Macedonians".

How can these people be anything other than Macedonian if this is what they were fighting and dying for against these neighbouring countries?

How can Bulgaria now claim a shared and common history with Goce Delcev if he was fighting ***against*** them?

Simon Tasievski

Macedonia: A History

Simon Tasievski

KALASH & THE HUNZA

In the last century (approx. 130 odd years ago), previously undiscovered tribes rarely ever visited by outsiders - the Hunza and the Kalash, were rediscovered living in the far remote and almost inaccessible Hindu Kush mountains of Northern Pakistan at a height of over 7,700m.

The Kalash and the Hunza living in the Hunza Valleys language is known as the Burushaski.
The Hindu Kush is an 800-kilometre-long mountain range on the Iranian Plateau in Central and South Asia to the west of the Himalayas. It stretches from central and eastern Afghanistan into northwestern Pakistan and far southeastern section of Tajikistan.
These people live in what today is called Pakistan, governing themselves and have their own independent laws.

The difficulty in getting to these people takes an arduous trek on average of around 8-9 days to get to, consisting of vehicles moving only at walking pace, walking, climbing, the use of pack horses, the crossing of gushing rivers etc. so it's no wonder that the surrounding peoples of the region during Alexander's campaign firmly believed that the Macedonians could actually fly, based on their remoteness and the extreme difficulty in getting there. (Read history on Alexanders army and the Sogdians)

Now what is incredibly interesting about these people is that they themselves claim to be the descendants of Alexander the

Great and his Macedonians! Macedonian soldiers that were either injured, too sick or too old to continue with Alexanders' campaign pressing on into India that had settled here, and these people have remained undisturbed for over 23 centuries.

These people have the same forms of art, wear the same clothing, have the same customs, and even speak a similar intelligible language to that of the Macedonians of today.

These people look nothing like others of their surrounding areas or countries. They don't look Asian, and they don't look Pakistani or Indian. These people are incredibly light skinned and basically all have either blue or green eyes and blonde/light hair.

The Kalash people, a white-skinned, blonde hair, blue-eyed tribe in the back

Photo by Hamid Hussain
www.mountaintravels.com

Macedonia: A History

Hunza Valley, Pakistan
Photography by Seth Lazar

Simon Tasievski

What is equally interesting is the very fact that in the 1990's, when the Greek Government was once again on their crusade to eradicate anything and everything that is Macedonian, that they approached these people and offered to build them a Greek school there.

You know, because Macedonians are Greek and always have been right?

The Hunza and the Kalash people promptly but kindly rejected their offer, stating that they were of Macedonian descent and not Greeks so why would they then want a Greek school there? Without saying anything, I can already see the smile on your face through the pages of this book. The Greek govt does *not* want this embarrassment to be known – yet it's been documented that it happened.

Riaz Haq 2008 – *"Led by Prince Ghazanfar Ali Khan and Princess Rani Atika, his parents the King and Queen of the Hunza visited Macedonia in 2008."*
""I am honoured to be in my country Macedonia", said Prince Ghazanfar Ali Khan of Hunza, as he arrived in Skopje, the capital of the Republic of Macedonia in July this year, according to Financial Times.
So what is the Wali of Hunza doing in Macedonia? It is hard to believe but true that Pakistan and Pakistanis figure prominently in the ongoing struggle for the inheritance of the legacy of Alexander the Great, and with it, Macedonia as a moniker. The prince and his wife, Princess Rani Atiqa and their entourage claim descent from Alexander the Great's conquering army, which reached their Hunza tribal homeland in northern Pakistan 23 centuries previously.

The fair-skinned, blue-eyed Hunza people, whose own accounts trace their descent to Alexander's march-weary troops, are renowned for their longevity and their high literacy rate, says the Financial Times story on Hunza. In the 1930s, scientists in Nazi Germany also combed the Himalayas in search of lost Aryan cousins.

In addition to the Macedonian prime minister and his cabinet, the Hunza delegation also met the Archbishop of Ohrid and Macedonia, HH Stefan, and Skopje Mayor Trifun Kostovski, according to Turkish Weekly Journal.
The delegation visited sites and towns throughout Macedonia and attended the renowned Galichnik Wedding. The Hunza visit was organized by Macedonian Institute for Strategic Research."

Balkan Insight July 11th, 2008 – "Skopje - A high delegation of the Hunza people from Northern Pakistan who claim to be descendants of the army of Alexander the Great, arrived on Friday in Skopje on a two week visit of Macedonia.

Led by Prince Ghazanfar Ali Khan and Princess Rani Atika, the delegation will see Macedonia's Prime Minister Nikola Gruevski and Archbishop Stefan from the Macedonian Orthodox Church upon their arrival.

The local NGO, Macedonian Institute for Strategic Research 16.9, on whose invitation they are arriving, argues that the Hunza people have much in common with today's Macedonians as they derive from the same origin.

The delegation includes a historian from the Hunza people who will travel across Macedonia to get acquainted with Macedonia's culture and tradition. They will also "visit the archaeological sites and see the artefacts dug from Macedonia," Marina Dojcinovska from The Institute told media on Thursday. The Institute said that according to the local linguist Ilija Casule, the Burushaski language that the Hunza people speak has some similarities to the Macedonian language. "Casule spent 12 years on this research," The Institute said.

According to a local Hunza legend they originate from the soldiers of Alexander the Great. Historians believe that during his reign from 336 - 323 B.C Alexander's kingdom reached far to the east covering the parts of today's Pakistan under the Himalaya Mountains where the Hunza people live."

Macedonia: A History

Simon Tasievski

POLITICS, OFFICIAL NAME CHANGES, FORCIBLE INTEGRATION, AND ANNEXATION OF LANDS

The names of over 804 Macedonian villages in Aegean Macedonia occupied by Greece in 1912 after the implementation of the Treaty of Bucharest, have forcibly been changed since 1926 and forward along with thousands of names of toponyms and geographical areas and places. Following the Treaty of Bucharest, the Macedonian place names that existed were gradually changed to Greek names, this included people's family and given names and was referred to as "Hellenization", as they were not - nor have ever been 'Hellenic' people.

On the 21st, October 1926 in the *"Official Gazette of Greece"* n.332 was announced the Law of obligatory change of the names of all settled places in the Aegean part of Macedonia. There exist to this day Macedonian place names all over Greece that weren't initially picked up in the thousands of name changes that were made during the 1920's. It was in the early 1900's that thousands of place names, roads, villages, towns, cities, bridges, rivers, mountains, and worst of all – on the gravestones of the dead, were all changed from Macedonian to Greek sounding names which has never occurred anywhere at any point in time in history, anywhere else in the world. This is an absolute atrocity of the very worst kind. Why would they even need changing you may ask yourself?

How systematically this measure was implemented is demonstrated by the fact that in a period of 10 years between

1918 to 1928, the names of 1,497 inhabited places alone were changed, not including the toponyms, bridges or rivers etc.

Voden, Lerin, Kostur, Solun as well as many others etc. *all* still show up on Google Maps with the original names to this very day!

Type into Google Maps *any* of the original place names and surprise surprise, it takes you to the newly named place that Greece had changed it to over 100 years ago.

I challenge you to try any of these and see for yourself.

Type Kostur and it will take you to Kastoria. Type Kukush and it will take you to Kilkis. Type Lerin and it will take you to Florina. Type Solun and it will take you to Thessalonika. Type Voden and it will take you to Edessa. Do it.

Type any of these original names into Google Maps and see for yourself!

Simon Tasievski

**These are the towns and villages alone, <u>not</u> including the roads, bridges, rivers, mountains etc.
Macedonian Names - [New Greek Name]**

Armensko [Alonas]
Balgarsko-Blatsa [Oksies]
Banica, Banitsa [Vevi] (Lerin region)
Barovica [Kastaneri]
Belotinci [Levkoia]
Ber
Berista [Ptelea]
Besvinia [Sfika]
Bituse [Parorion]
Bizovo [Megaloplatanos]
Blace [Ahladia]
Blaci [Oksies]
Bobchor [Pimenikon]
Bobista [Verga]
Boevo [Katsanovo]
Bogacko [Ajos Nikolaos]
Bojmica [Aksiupolis]
Boresnica [Palestra]
Boriani [Ajos Atanasios]
Borislav [Periklia]
Borovo [Potami]
Bozec [Atira]
Brest [Akrolimnion]
Bresteni [Kria Nera]
Breznica [Vatohorion]
Bruhovo [Kokina]
Buf [Akrita]
Bugarievo [Karavias]
Buk [Paranestion]
Bukovik [Oksia]

Bukovo [Oksia]
Bulamasli [Akakies]
Bultista [Profitis Ilias]
Butkovo [Kerkini]
Chavdar [Psomotopi]
Chegan [Meteora]
Chereshnitsa [Polikerason]
Chereshovo [Pagoneri]
Cherkovian [K1idohor]
Chernak [Strotis]
Cherna-reka [Karpi]
Chernova [Fitia]
Chernovishta [Mavrokampos]
Chetirok [Mezopotama]
Chiflik [Triha]
Chushuligovo [Anagenizis]
Dabovo [Valtotopi]
Dambeni [Dendrohori]
Darovo [Ketrokampos]
Demir Hisar [Sidirokastron]
Derveni [Akritodohori]
Dobrolishta [Kalohori]
Dolno Rodivo [Kato Korifi]
Dolno Garbali [Kato Surmena]
Dolno Kleshtino [Kato Klene]
Dolno Kotori [Kato Idruza]
Dolno Pozarsko
Dovista [Papas]
Dracevo [Levkotea]
Dragomanci [Apsalos]
Dragomir [Vapsiohori]
Dragos [Zevgolatio]
Drama
Dramendzik [Drakontion]

Dranic [Antifilipi]
Dravunista [Geraki]
Dremiglava [Drimos]
Drenoveny [Kranionas]
Drenovo [Glikoneri]
Drenovo [Monastiraki]
Dreveno [Pili]
Druska [Drosia]
Dudular [Djavata]
Dupiak [Dispilion]
Durgutli [Nigdi]
Dutli [Eleon]
Dzuma [Amigdala]
Egri Dere [Kalitea]
Ehatli [Kavalaris]
Ekshi-su [Ksino Nero]
Elesnica [Fea Pitra]
Elevo [Lakia]
Elsen [Karperi]
Ezerec [Petropulaki]
Fetista [Pola Nera]
Fotinista [Fotini]
Fotovista [Valtohoro]
Frankovica [Ermakia]
Fuceli [Semeli]
Fustani [Evropos]
Galista [Omorfoklisia]
Garbasel [Kastanies]
Garipci [Hloronomos]
Garljanl [Hionaton]
Gaskarla [Kalohori]
Gavalanci [Valtudi]
Gavrista [Dorotea]
Gedi-Dermen [Eptomili]

German [Shistolitos]
Gevsekli [Rematia]
Gjulobasi [Pikrolimni]
Gjumenic [Stiva]
Gjundzeli [Vamvakuza]
Gjupcevo [Gipsohori]
Gjuredzik [Granitis]
Gjuvezna [Asiros]
Globostica [Kalohorio]
Gola [Korifes]
Golem Besik [Megali Volvi]
Golem Sevidrik [Megalokampos]
Golisani [Levkadia]
Golo-selo [Gimna]
Gorenci [Korisos]
Gorna Nuska [Ano Dafnudi]
Gorni Postular [Ano Apostoli]
Gornica [Kalivrisi]
Gornicevo [Ke1i]
Gorno Garbali [Ano Surmena]
Gorno Karadzakjoj [Monoklisia]
Gorno Klestino [Ano Klene]
Gorno Krusare [Ekso Asladohori]
Gorno Krusovo [Ano Kervilion]
Gorno Papratsko [Ano Fterias]
Gorno Pozarsko [Ano Lutraki]
Gorno Rodivo [Ano Korifi]
Gorno Selo [Ano Vermion]
Govlishta [Krokos]
Gradishte [Kiros]
Gradobori [Pentalofos]
Granci [Ftelia]
Granichevo [Krioneri]
Grazhden [Vronteron]

Gropino [Voltolivado]
Gugovo [Virita]
Gurbesh [Agriosikia]
Hadji-bejlik [Vironia]
Hadzl-bajramli [Teodosia]
Harava [Polikilon]
Harman-kjoj [Stadmos]
Harsovo [Herson]
Hasanovo [Mezohori]
Haznatar [Hrizohorafa]
Hedzik [Fikiros]
Hedzik [Filiros]
Hodzovo [Karidia]
Holeva [Amision]
Hrupishta [Argu Oresticon]
Ilezli [Inoi]
Indzes [Eratni]
Ineovo [Avrini]
Isirli [Platanotopos]
Istrane [Perasma]
Izbishta [Agriokerasia]
Izglibi [Poria]
Izvor [Pigi]
Jadzilar [Ksilokeratia]
Janes [Metaliko]
Janikia [Askos]
Janoveni [Janohori]
Janozli [Karpofonon]
Jaramzli [Ajdonia]
Javor [Diamezon]
Javorjani [Platani]
Javornica [Nea Kuklina]
Jundzular [Kimina]
Kadinovo [Galatas]

Kajacali [Triadi]
Kajali [Vrahia]
Kajljar [Ptolemes]
Kalevista [Kali Vrisi]
Kalinovo [Sutojaneika]
Kaljani [Eani]
Kamenik [Petrias]
Kandza [Aniksia]
Kapinjani [Eksaplatanos]
Kara-bej [Karna]
Kara-bunar [Angelofrori] (Solun region)
Kara-bunar [Mavroneri] (Kukus region)
Kara-bunar [Mavropigi] (Kozani region)
Kara-cali [Kaliroj] (Seres region)
Kara-cali [Mavrodendri] (Ber region)
Kara-cali [Mavrovatos] (Drama region)
Kara-cukali [Kardia]
Karad-ilar [Drepanon]
Karadza [Evangelizmos]
Karadza-kjoj [Tolos] (Drama region)
Karadza-kjoj [Kartera] (Lagadina region)
Karadzova [Elafohori]
Karagac [Mavrodendri]
Kara-kjoj [Kalegiri]
Kara-mahala [Koronia]
Karamanli [Ajos Kozmos]
Karandzilari [Zarkadia]
Kara-tepe [Mavrolofos]
Karcovo [Koridohori]
Kardzalar [Adendron]
Karilova [Zardadion]
Karladovo [Milias]
Karlakovo [Mikropolis]
Karrcista [Polianemon]

Katranica [Pirgi]
Katun [Dipotama]
Kavadzik [Levkadi]
Kavakli [Egiros] (Drama region)
Kavakli [Perintos] (Kukus region)
Kazanovo [Kotili]
Kiklova [Kastanies]
Klabucista [Poliplatanos]
Kladorobi [Kladorahi]
Klepusna [Agriani]
Klisali [Prositis]
Kobalica [Kokinogia]
Kocan [Rizana]
Kocana [Perea]
Kocani [Kostani]
Kokova [Polidendri]
Kolarica [Manjaki]
Komarjan [Kimaria]
Konica [Pevki]
Konikovo [Stiba]
Konomladi [Makrohori]
Konsko [Talakini]
Konuf [Elos]
Korcak [Mirini]
Kornisor [Kromni]
Kosinec [Jeropigi]
Kosinovo [Polipetron]
Kostur [Kastoria]
Kosturjani [Ksifonia]
Kozani
Kozusani [Filotia]
Kramca [Mezovunos]
Kramca [Mezovunos]
Kranista [Dendrari]

Krastali [Korona]
Krecovo [Ajos Jorgios]
Krepesino [Atrapos]
Kroncelevo [Kerasies]
Krusari [Ampelies]
Krusoradi [Ahlada]
Krusovo [Ahladohori]
Kuckari [Galini]
Kuckoveni [Parama]
Kukus [Kulkis]
Kula [Paleokastron]
Kulakia [Halastra]
Kumanic [Daston]
Kumanicevo [Litia]
Kurcova [Liebra]
Kusovo [Kokina]
Kutles [Verdina]
Kutuger [Kesariana]
Labanica [Ajos Dimitrios]
Ladza [Terma]
Lagina [Litokastron]
Lagino [Triantafilia]
Lakavica [Mikromilia]
Lanki [Mikrolimni]
Latrovo [Hortero]
Lehovo [Krasohori]
Lelovo [Ajos Antonios]
Lembed [Evkarpia]
Lerin [Florina]
Leskovec [Leptocaries]
Leskovo [Tria Elata]
Lestan [Farasinon]
Leveni [Vasiludi]
Liban [Skaloti]

Libanovo [Eginion]
Licista [Polikarpos]
Likovan [Ksilopolis]
Likovista [Likojani]
Lipus [Filira]
Lise [Ohiron]
Ljubetino [Pedino]
Ljumnica [Skra]
Losnica [Germas]
Lovca [Akrohori] (Seres region)
Lovca [Kalikarpon] (Drama region)
Lozanovo [Palefiton]
Lozica [Mezolofos]
Ludovo [Kria Nera]
Lugunci [Langadia]
Lukovic [Sotira]
Luvradi [Skieron]
Macukovo [Evzoni]
Mahaledzik [Milorema]
Malak Besik [Mikra Volvi]
Malko-Osmanli [Kosmiti]
Malovica [Hiliolustro]
Markovjani [Markohori]
Mavrovo [Mavrohori] (Kostur region)
Mavrovo [Mavruda] (Lagadina region)
Mec [Mezi]
Medovo [Milionas]
Menteseli [Eli]
Mentesli [Moshuia]
Merjan [Ligaria]
Mertatevo [Ksirotopos]
Meseli [Drias]
Mezdurek [Melisurgio]
Milovo [Megali Gefira]

Mirovo [Eliniko]
Mokreni [Variko]
Mokro [Polikrinos]
Morafca [Antigonia]
Mramor [Kapetanudi]
Mrsna [Gonimon]
Muncino [Lekani]
Munuhi [Mavrotalasa]
Muralar [Pelagros]
Muralti [Skopos]
Murodonli [Mirovliton]
Mursali [Monokaridia]
Musacali [Aetofolia]
Muselim [Aedonokastron]
Muska [Kudunia]
Mutulovo [Metaksohori]
Negocani [Niri]
Nered [Polipotamos]
Nesram [Nestorion]
Neveska [Nemfeon]
Nevoleni (Dolno) [Vamvaria]
Nevoleni (Gorno) [Skopia]
Nigoslav [Nikoklia]
Nivica [Psarades]
Novi grad [Ve Gora]
Novo Selo [Korfula] (Kostur region)
Novo Selo [Nehorion] (Lagadina region)
Novoselci [Joromilos]
Novoselsko [Nea Komi]
Obor [Aravizos]
Obsirena [Etnikon]
Okcilar [Toksote]
Oladzak [Platamon]
Olista [Melisotopos]

Omotsko [Livdadotopos]
Orchovica [Pevkodazos]
Organdzilar [Sapeon]
Orizarci [Rizia]
Orizari [Rizarion]
Orljak [Strimonikon]
Orman [Kato-Levki]
Ormanli [Dasohori] (Seres region)
Ormanli [Polikarpos] (Drama region)
Ormanovo [Dasero]
Orovo [Karie]
Osani [Lnoi]
Oshchima (see Ostima) [Trigonon]
Osin [Argangelos]
Osljani [Ajos Fotini]
Oslovo [Panagica]
Osmanica [Kalos Agros]
Osmanli [Hrisokastron] (Pravista region)
Osmanli [Neromilos] (Halkidiki region)
Ostica [Mikromilia]
Ostima (see Oshchima) [Trigonon]
Ostrovo [Arnisa]
Palmes [Kastanusa]
Papli [Levkonas]
Paprat [Pontokerasia]
Pastrovo [Kalikrunon]
Patele [Pontokerasia]
Paticino [Patima]
Pazarlar [Agora]
Pazarli [Dikorfon] (Halkidiki region)
Pazarli [Melansion] (Kukus region)
Pejkovo [Ajos Markoc]
Pelkati [Monopili]
Pemovali [Aja Ekaterini]

Simon Tasievski

Pesjak [Amudara]
Pesocnica [Amohori]
Petgas [Pentalofon]
Petorica [Hrizohori]
Planica [Fiska]
Plasnicevo [Kria Vrisi]
Plesevica [Kolhiki]
Plevna [Petruza]
Plugar [Ludias]
Pocep [Margarita]
Podgorjani [Podohorion]
Poljani [Polikarpi]
Popovo [Miriotiton]
Porna [Gazoros]
Postol [Pela]
Potores [Aja Kiriaki]
Pozdivista [Halara]
Prahna [Aspro]
Prebadiste [Sosandra]
Pribojna [Vunohoron]
Prosenik [Skotusa]
Prosocen [Pirsopolis]
Provista [Palekomi]
Pselsko [Kipseli]
Psora [Ipsilon]
Puljovo [Termopigi]
Purlida [Konhilia]
Radigoze [Aja Ana]
Radomir [Asvestario]
Radovista [Rodjani]
Radovo [Haropo]
Radovo [Krateron]
Radunista [Kria Vrisi]
Ragjan [Vati]

Rahmanli [Antigoni] (Kukus region)
Rahmanli [Eleuza] (Lerin region)
Rahmanli [Galina] (Kozani region)
Rahovica [Marmaras]
Rahovo [Mezorahi] (Drama region)
Rahovo [Rahia] (Ber region)
Rajkovci [Kapnotopos]
Rakistan [Katahloron]
Rakita [Olimpias]
Ramel [Rahona]
Ramna [Mono1iti] (Dojran region)
Ramna [Omalo] (Enidze Vardar region)
Ranislav [Agati]
Rapes [Drepani]
Rasovo [Limon]
Ravenia [Makriplagi]
Ravica [Kalifiton]
Ravna [Lsoma]
Razenik [Haradra]
Rehimli [Mezia]
Resen [Sitaria]
Resilovo [Haritomeni]
Retini [Riakon]
Revani [Dipotamia]
Rizovo [Rizo]
Robovo [Rodonas]
Rudino [Aloras]
Rulja [Katohori]
Rula [Kottas]
Rumbi [Lemos]
Rum-Saret [Vromosiria]
Rupel [Klidion]
Rusilovo [Ksantogia]
Rusovo [Makroliti]

Ruzeni [Rizohori]
Sabotsko [Adrea]
Sadina [Karavi]
Sakafca [Evadohori]
Sakulevo [Marina]
Salamanli [Galikos]
Samokovov [Domatia]
Saraci [Falara]
Saradza [Valtohori]
Saraj [Sholarion]
Sarajli [Palatianon]
Sarakinovo [Sarakini]
Sari-gjol [Kriston]
Sarmusalari [Kokinohori]
Sar-pazar [Antofiton]
Sborsko [Revkoton]
Sehovo [Idomeni]
Seljani [Mezorena]
Semasi [Kremaston]
Sendelcevo [Sandali]
Seneleli [Rodokipos]
Seremeti [Fanarion]
Serermli [Kserovrisi]
Seres
Seslovo [Sevaston]
Setina [Skopos]
Setoma [Kefalari]
Sevendekli [Eptalofon]
Severjani [Vorino]
Sfilci [Hromion]
Sicevo [Sidirohori]
Siderova [Mezovuni]
Sivri [Nea Mahala]
Skrizevo [Skopia]

Slalina [Hrisi] (Voden region)
Slatina [Hrisi] (Kostur region)
Slimista [Milica]
Sliveni [Koromilia]
Smol [Mikron Dasos]
Smurdes [Krustalopigi]
Sokolovo [Parapotomos]
Solun/Salonika [Thessaloniki]
Sosuri [Nimfi]
Spanci [Fanos] (Lerin region)
Spanci [Latomi] (Kukus region)
Spatjovo [Kimezis]
Spirlitovo [Plagiari]
Sporlita [Elefina]
Srebreni [Asprogia]
Starcista [Peritori]
Staricani [Lacomala]
Statica [Melas]
Stavrovo [Stavrodromi]
Straista [Ida]
Strezovo [Argirupolis]
Strupino [Likostomon]
Subas-kjoj [Neon Suli]
Sufilar [Angelohori] (Halkidiki region)
Suflar [Angelohori] (Pravista region)
Suha-banja [Ksilotros] (Nigrita region)
Suha-banja [Paliotros] (Lake Tahino)
Sujudzuk [Lima]
Sulovo [Amaranta]
Sveta Gora [Mount Athos]
Sveta Nedelja [Aja Kiriaki]
Sveta Petka [Aja Paraskevi] (Lerin region)
Tagramisevo [Idromilos]
Tarlis [Sidirohori]

Tarnovo [Ankatoton]
Tarsje [Trivunon]
Tehovo [Karidias]
Tekeli [Sindos]
Tekri [Paralimni]
Tekri-Vermisli [Kserorevma]
Telkili [Petralona]
Tikisli [Talasia]
Tikveni [Kalokinton]
Tiolista [Tihion]
Tohova [Palionelines]
Toilar [Peristeri]
Toma [Avgo]
Topci [Gefira]
Topcilar [Ajos Dimitrios]
Topljani [Jorgjani]
Topola [Kiriaki]
Topoljan [Hrizo]
Topolovo [Nea Tiroloi]
Trebeno [Kardia]
Trebolec [Tripolis]
Trepista [Ajos Hristoforos]
Tresino [Ormai]
Trifulcevo [Trifili]
Trihovista [Kamiohori]
Tuhol [Pevkos]
Tukica [Trias]
Tukovo [Leptokaria]
Tumba [Emvolos]
Turbes [Makriotisa]
Turceli [Trakiko]
Turje [Korifi]
Turmanli [Rodonia]
Tursko selo [Milopotamos]

Tusilovo [Stadis]
Tusin [Aetohiri]
Udzana [Komninon]
Ugurli [Peristereon]
Vageni [Sevastia]
Valcista [Domeron]
Valgaci [Kampohoro]
Valkojanovo [Liki]
Valkovo [Hrisokefolos]
Varbjani [Itea]
Vardarovci [Aksiohori]
Vardino [Limnotopos]
Vardrista [Milotopos]
Varlankza [Agroniri]
Vartokop [Skidra]
Vartolom [Ajos Vartolomeos]
Vates [Nea Epivate]
Vazme [Ekzohori]
Veldziler [Dimaros]
Velisti [Levkopigi]
Verzjani [Kato Psihiko]
Vestica [Angelohori]
Vetrina [Neo Petrici]
Veznik [Monikos]
Virlan [Anavrito]
Vishani [Vissinia]
Visocan [Ksiropotamos]
Visoka [Osa]
Vitan [Votani]
Vitivjani [Polifiton]
Vitovo [Delta]
Vladikovo [Oropedion]
Vladovo [Agras]
Voden [Edesa]

Vojvodina [Spilia]
Volcisia [Idoea]
Volovot [Nea Santa]
Voronos [Kikomidinon]
Vosova [Sfikia]
Vostarani [Meliti]
Zarnovo [Kato Nevrokopion]
Zabrdeni [Lofi] (Lerin region)
Zabrdeni [Melantion] (Kostur region)
Zagoricani [Vasilias]
Zahardzi [Tagarades]
Zarovo [Nikopolis]
Zdralci [Ampelokipi]
Zdravik [Draviskos]
Zelegozdi [Pentavrison]
Zelenice [Sklitron]
Zelin [Heliodendron]
Zensko [Ginekokastron]
Zerveni [Ajos Antonios]
Zhelevo [Andartikon]
Ziljanovo [Nea Zihni]
Zimbjul Mahala [Pevkolofos]
Zorbatovo [Mikro Monastiri]
Zulica [Spitea]
Zupanista [Anolevki]

Simon Tasievski

MAP DISPLAYING THE VILLAGES AND TOWN NAME CHANGES

TOTALLY NORMAL RIGHT?!

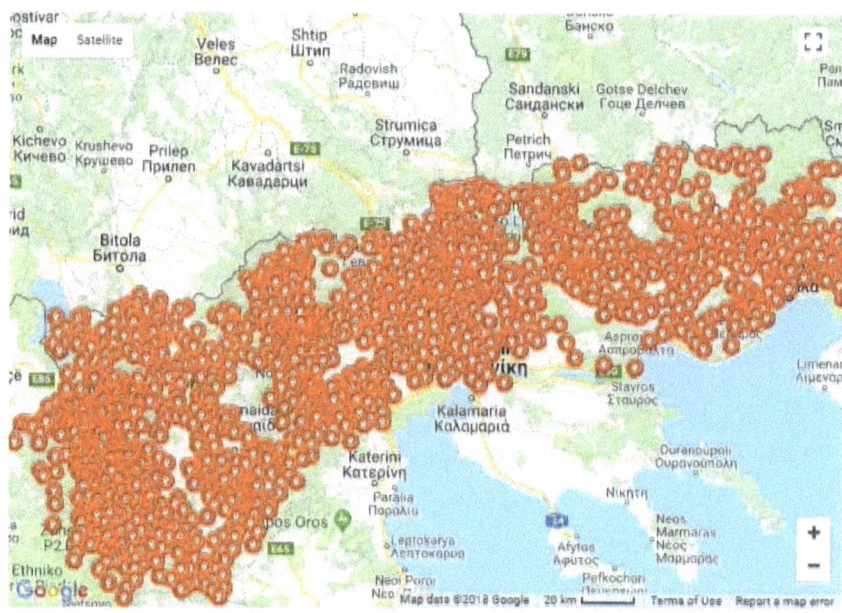

1927 Greek Government Legislative Edict:
The Greek Government Gazette declared that "there are not any non-Greek people in Greece".

This was part of a process whereby all the names of Macedonian villages, towns, regions, rivers, streets, mountain ranges etc. were changed, together with the surnames of ethnic Macedonians, into Greek versions.

1934-1941 Military Dictatorship in Greece:
At its height, the Fascists regime **prohibits** the speaking of the Macedonian language. People were forcibly made to change their names to Greek sounding names or face torture and exile to hostile Greek island prisons if they didn't. The Macedonian language was simply outlawed and forbidden. There are countless eye witness documented books and references of Greek soldiers that would sit underneath windows of houses in villages and towns where one would assume they were safe, and if they (the soldiers) heard anyone speaking the Macedonian language, they would be dragged out and force-fed castor oil to drink, tortured and even imprisoned to scare the population into "forgetting" where they are really from and who they really are, because now they are 'Greek'.

The whole history of Europe is connected with Macedonia, which is why they all try to deny it as it would disrupt their narrative of history. Winston Churchill has famously stated that "the Balkans produce more history than they can consume."
But that is only a short paraphrase of his statement that is today being used against the Macedonians, the full statement actually says:
"The whole history of Europe is connected with Macedonia, Europe divided Macedonia in 1913, during the First World War the biggest battles were fought on Macedonian territory. Attempts to assimilate the Macedonians were fortunately unsuccessful. Eventually in one part of Macedonia the Macedonians created their own State within Yugoslavia. But such a reason frightened Greece and made an exodus over the Macedonians, the Macedonians are descendants of Philip and Alexander and have the right to live in their own country. But I am afraid that their rich history in the future will bring them too many problems that Bulgaria and Greece will impose on them

because they are afraid of the existence of Macedonia and the Macedonians." Winston Churchill.

After the partition of Macedonia in 1913, the 51% region that the recently formed Greece had annexed (literally meaning that it was never theirs to even begin with) was originally at first called "occupied territories", Hmm funny that wouldn't you agree?! Then, was later renamed to the "northern territories", then once again to "northern Greece".

To provide context, 51% of Macedonian territory accounts for a little over 67,000km^2, which is still larger than 135 out of the 195 countries currently in the world today. That is over 69% of countries that currently exist so yes, it's a huge deal and also no wonder that Greece is fighting tooth and nail to prevent it from being returned to its rightful owners.

The name Macedonia and anything that *was* Macedonian was forbidden under Greek law to ever be mentioned. For almost 100 years it was repeated over and over again that "Macedonia does not exist". It's only since the late 1980's when it was evident that the breakup of Yugoslavia was imminent and that the Republic of Macedonia was to once again become a free nation, only *then* did the Greek attitude change and humorously do an entire backflip, as they knew very well that they were occupying foreign land that simply did not and had never belonged to them. Only *then* did the chant miraculously change from 100+ years of "Macedonia does not exist", to "Macedonia exists, and it is Greek and has always been Greek".

Is anyone with a sane mind honestly taking any of this seriously?

In the early decades of the 1900's after the annexation of the 51% of Macedonian lands that was forcibly assimilated, the Greek state installed night classes at the local schools to teach the population the "Greek" language.
Why would anyone, anywhere, need to 'teach' the people a language from a place that apparently either never existed, or, had always been a part of for thousands of years?

In the 1920's, millions of people exchanges were conducted with Turkey with Greece to ethnically cleanse the Macedonian people from the Greek annexed Macedonian region. The Greek govt. offered to exchange the Muslim Turks that had remained from Ottoman domination after the empire fell, with the Christian Turks from Asia Minor promising them citizenship, free homes, free education, and free agricultural assistance etc. as long as they swore allegiance to the Greek State.
(doesn't seem sketchy at all by any means and is *totally* normal everywhere, right? Right?!?...)

These were the very same homes of the Macedonian people the Greek govt slaughtered or drove out.
The entire exercise was designed to replace the Macedonian population, with "Greeks". Many Macedonians so poor and so vulnerable, were left with no choice but to accept the Greek demands – yet they never forgot who they were, never forgot their language and remain there to this day. There is an abundance of books on this from the Macedonians in Greece.

 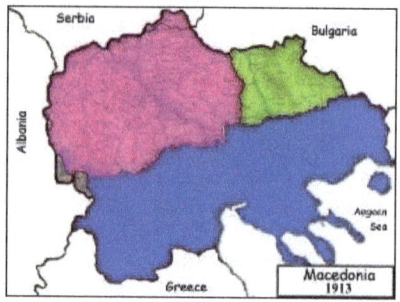

Macedonia Undivided   Partition of Macedonia in 1913

In the information by the Ambassador of the Kingdom of Serbs Croats and Slovenes from London (1926) it was said that during the visit of the Dictator Pangalos to Lerin (modern day Florina near the current Macedonian/Greek border) that he gave 14 million drachmas for the construction of 80 new schools prevalently in the settlements inhabited by the Macedonian population. In the comment regarding the information of the Ambassador it was said: "The whole of this plan of work clearly demonstrates the intention of the Greek authority as quick as possible to erase the issue related to the Macedonian minority from the right side of the river Vardar". The terror was particularly considered within the policy of the Greek state regarding the quick denationalization and assimilation of the Macedonians in the Aegean part of Macedonia.

Besides the repression carried out by the state administrative organs, the teaching staff, the Greek priests and so on, numerous para-military formations were also formed with a task to terrorize the Macedonians - especially the rural population who were much easier to manipulate than the city dwellers. Among various organizations of this type, the following names remained traced deep in the memory of the Macedonians from the Aegean part of Macedonia: "The Greek-Macedonian fist" (formed on the 27th January 1926); National Youth organization (well-known under the abbreviation-EEE); "Pavlos Melas"; The National League of Greece known under the name of "Steel Helms" and others.

A paradigm for the terrorist actions of these and other similar organizations represents the edict by the "The Greek-Macedonian fist" of January 27, 1926, in which it was ordered the Greek language to be spoken in all public places, at restaurants, during the trade negotiations, at meetings, during meals, weddings and the required information from the state administrative institutions to be formulated in Greek. All those that would not act in compliance with this order would be declared traitors and they would be most severely sentenced.

Considering everything, the Greek terror towards Macedonians in the Aegean part of Macedonia was characterized with tremendous xenophobia. The writings of various foreigners that were visiting Greece or more precisely, the Aegean part of Macedonia are the best proof of the Greek attitude towards the Macedonians. "The Greeks," wrote an English publicist of 1928, "not only hound all the alive Macedonians, that are sometimes called "Bulgarophones" and sometimes "Slavophones", but also all those passed away whose graves are found all over Macedonia. They do not let them even die in peace because they wipe out the titles written on the crosses in Macedonian letters, they take the bones out of the graves and burn them".

On the 15th, July 1937 in the "Greek state newspaper" was announced a decree in which the use of the Macedonian names of villages and cities were forbidden in public and private communication.

I wonder how this could even be possible if "Macedonia is always Greek!?"

A close friend of Metaxas, Godzomanis, testifies how strong that pressure was. He had courage in front of the dictator to expose in written form his personal disagreements with the authority's operations: "to be addressed insulting words, he wrote, for instance, to an elderly man and woman or to be deported to police stations just because they do not speak Greek well is something that could not be justified as a system. This responsibility of the history and of the state regarding one reality, in the concrete case is transferred to one innocent individual. The practicing of such measures by one state administrative organ is considered vicious and hostile and it compromises the state in the eyes of the citizen and the citizen started hating it. In any case this practice cannot be interpreted as a method of the Greek language teaching." And exactly this hate towards the methods of the Greek assimilation policy remained deeply in the memory of the Macedonian people and is transmitted from generation to generation.

Here is one example from thousands of them, which was registered in the resolution text of a protest meeting organized by the refugees from the Aegean part of Macedonia: "The terrorist groups by giving castor oil to everyone who speaks the Macedonian language will remain forever present in the memory of the Macedonian people from Aegean Macedonia".

This actually happened...

9th September 1944: the Germans calculated that considering the circumstances it would have been much more useful to accomplish the idea of "Independent Macedonia" under leadership of Ivan Mihajlov. Hitler signed the order for the creation and reunification of an "Independent Macedonia" on September 5th, 1944. For the implementation of this idea, he appointed Dr. Garben and the German Consul in Skopje, Arthur Vite. On the 6th September 1944, Ivan Mihajlov arrived in Skopje and immediately started with the preparations related to the declaration of the "Independent Macedonia". Unfortunately, his supporters informed him that the divided Macedonian state had already been created and that it was late to declare "Independent Macedonia". Depressed and deluded that he had not managed to declare the "Independent Macedonia" and under the protectorate of Germany, on the 7th September 1944 in the evening hours, Ivan Mihajlov left Skopje. With the failure of the idea of "Independent Macedonia", the German Military Headquarters that was politically subordinate to Dr. Hermann Neubacher became in charge of the safety of the Macedonian territory. Due to the deterioration of the situation on the fronts, on the 4th October 1944 Hitler ordered an unconditional withdrawal of all German formations from Greece and from Macedonia. Why would these two countries be named separately if they were the same thing and the same people as Greece loves to claim?

The Greek Civil War where the vast majority of fighters were the native Macedonians, who were all purposely placed in the front line was actually an ethnic cleansing exercise with the Greek communist party falsely promising them reunification with the rest of Macedonia. This was done under Zahariadis and Markos. (Zahariadis was born in Thrace and a native Thracian, only moving to 'Greece' in 1924. Markos was born near Ankara in Asia Minor, deposited into the northern provinces in the 1920's, both were incentivised by the Greek Govt with lands and power to rid the northern province of Macedonians). I wonder what that reunification the Greek government spoke of could have possibly meant? This was simply a guise to entice the Macedonian people to go fight and die out so there would be no more Macedonians left.

There technically by all means and purposes should have been no more wars immediately following WW2, considering it being "the war to end all wars" so why did this happen and who seems to benefit most from it?

Greece benefits from it, that's who.

During the XII CPG Central Committee Plenary session, held on June 25th – 27th 1945, in his political speech, Zahariadis said: "We are against any change in the 1939 boundaries by use of force no matter where that force comes from. The only democratic principle we recognize is the principle of self-determination of peoples. This principle applies to the Dodecanese, Cyprus, and North Epirus. At the same time, we strive to implement another democratic principle for the national minorities, the principle of equality and respect. That principle should also apply to the Macedonian minority, to regulate our relations with the northern Balkan republics in a friendly manner." (See: "Rizospastis" July 17, 1945.) So, Macedonia apparently doesn't exist, or is an invention of Tito in 1945, yet here we have the General Secretary of the Communist Party of Greece (KKE) from 1931 to 1956, documented as speaking of a Macedonian minority.

During the Greek civil war in the 1940's under the guise of "humanitarian aid" made by the Queen Frederika of Greece to safeguard the children, almost 30,000 children aged 3-14 were exiled and forcibly removed from their parents and sent by trains to Czechoslovakia, Hungary, Romania, Poland, Russia, as well as many other countries. A little strange wouldn't you think considering that only the children from Greek occupied Macedonia (Aegean Macedonia) were taken, who were also very far away from where any of the action of this war had actually taken place which was mainly down south in Athens. None of the Greek children from what we refer to as "Greece proper" were taken.

One Macedonian "mother" was charged with looking after 20 children at a time. Those under 3 who were too young to speak, know or understand any better remained (as they could be easily manipulated into 'loyal Greeks' through schooling and indoctrination), and those older than 14 who could be armed and forced to fight for the communist party of Greece that were sent on purpose to die in an unwinnable war were exempt.

Why did the Greek government enact the edict 106.841 / 5-1-83, to repatriate only "Greeks by birth" for the return of these children and families after this civil war had ended?

The Macedonians that refused to change their names to Greek names or sign papers claiming that they were "Greek by ethnos" still to this day cannot return to Greece even in 2025.

Where were these 30,000 children supposedly born then? Are they not human?

Why can't they return and why are they banned from re-entry into 'Greece'?

These are the deca begalci (refugee children) we have all heard the tales of - only they aren't simply 'tales' but a fact of what actually happened and banned by Greek Law to this very day.

Founders of Democracy hey!?

On February 21st 1947, the British Government informed the U.S. Government that as of March 31st 1947, due to economic difficulties, it could no longer assist Greece. The U.S. government had estimated that if it failed to meet its UK obligations to Greece, it would face greater consequences in the future. To prevent this from happening, U.S. President Truman announced his doctrine known as the Truman Doctrine where he granted Greece $300 million to protect the Athens regime and keep the monarchy intact. It was in the UK and US's best interests to have strong political influence over the ports of

Greece (and the annexed Macedonian ports), as the Cold War also started in 1947, and they did not want Russia having any access to the Aegean or subsequent Mediterranean Seas.

Germanos Karavangelis was born in 1866 in the village Stipsi on the island of Lesbos. He graduated from the University of Munich with great success and his desire was to devote himself to education as a professor of theology, but at the request of the Greek government in 1900 he was appointed Metropolitan of the Kostur Diocese (modern day Kastoria). In a short time after that, Karavangelis created a whole network of priests, teachers, and others all throughout the Kostur villages. He used bribes and golden liras to bribe his way and to get what he wanted. In his memoirs, he described in detail his actions and cruel methods he used working with Pavlos Melas in Hellenising the Macedonians. Pavlos Melas, chief and organizer of the Greek Andart detachments, appeared in Macedonia in 1901.

In March 1977, the Greek newspaper "Kathimerini" reporting on the European Parliament's initiative to record minorities and their cultural rights in Europe, also mentioning the reports written by Fon Stoutenberg and Coopers, said that: "five minorities exist in Greece, among which are the Macedonians, who in addition to speaking the official Greek language also speak four other languages: Turkish, Albanian, Vlach and Macedonian. Of all the Greek MPs, only Filinis, an independent MP, had the courage to confirm that it was true that all the mentioned minorities really did live in Greece"

The platform of the Communist Party Yugoslavia (CPY) in Macedonia was defined on the basis of the historical ambitions of the Macedonian people for liberation and independence. They were incorporated into the declaration of the CPY (in the spring 1939) titled: "Communist Party of Yugoslavia and the

Macedonian national issue". The fundamental point of this declaration was as follows: "The Macedonians represent a separate nation in the Balkans, they are not Greek, nor Serbs or Bulgarians, and without an absolute freedom of the Macedonian people the consolidation of Yugoslavia could not be imagined".

I thought that Macedonians never existed according to Greece? Or, that Macedonia was only a part of the 3 neighbouring countries being Serbia, Greece and Bulgaria - despite written history of Macedonia, a Macedonian nation and Macedonian people existing over 4,000 years ago when the words Yugoslavia, Serbia, Greece or Bulgaria didn't even exist or had ever been thought of.

Simon Tasievski

THE ROSETTA STONE

The Rosetta Stone is a giant stone of black granite that was discovered in the Nile delta of Egypt in 1799 that was written in 3 languages. The top was Egyptian Hieroglyphics. The middle was an "unknown language" that they referred to as "Demotic Egyptian" (even though this language is nowhere to be seen in any of the ancient monuments in Egypt, in Pyramids, on temples etc.), and the bottom was written in "Ancient Greek" (Koine).

The discovery of this stone was how they were able to translate and understand the ancient Egyptian Hieroglyphics, as the 3 languages were there one above the other and then used the Koine language from the bottom to decipher what the Egyptian Hieroglyphics at the top actually meant. Finally, after centuries all the Hieroglyphics on ancient monuments had a story to tell, but it was that unknown middle script that seemed to puzzle even the smartest of code breakers.

In 2005 after years of research, Tome Bosevski MASA & Aristotel Tentov FEEIT published a paper on the Rosetta Stone that went out to academia, providing evidence that the middle script was not a form of unknown or demotic Egyptian at all, but rather the Ancient Macedonian script which was read from right to left! Please see below for some short excerpts from their study:

"The Rosetta Stone is one of the best-known textual artifacts from ancient Egypt and has been the object of a great number of studies and much research in the scholarly world of this field. It has its name because the location where it was excavated, that is Rosetta, i.e. El-Rashid in Arabic. It was discovered by a

French soldier who had been working on excavating fortifications for the needs of Napoleon's army during his campaign in Egypt in the year 1799, after a short military clash with the English army, when he won the battle, a peace treaty was signed in Alexandria in 1802. In accordance with the regulations of this peace treaty all the goods and artifacts possessed by the French army became the property of the British. Based on this, the Rosetta Stone was moved to England where it still is today and is one of the best-known exhibits at the British Museum in London. The Rosetta Stone is a stone of black granite.

The importance of the Rosetta Stone and the interest it has aroused in the scientific and scholarly world are based on the fact that special decree had been inscribed on it, which, according to contemporary scholarship, was issued by the priests in order to glorify the pharaoh Ptolemy V Epiphany Eucharist one year after his coronation, more precisely, according to present-day calendar on 27th March 196 B.C. The special interest arises because this decree was written in three different scripts: in hieroglyphs, in so-called demotic script and in the ancient Greek alphabet. Based on the text written in the ancient Greek alphabet, in 1822 the well-known French scientist Champollion deciphered the hieroglyphic script using the ancient Egyptian language for wiring for sound.

According to the perceptions of contemporary science, as well as the text being written in three scripts, two languages had been used: ancient Egyptian, in the text written with hieroglyphs and in the demotic script, and ancient Greek in the text written in ancient Greek script. The thesis that three scripts and three languages are used on the Rosetta Stone was widely accepted until the beginning of the 20th century. Due to the difficulties in determining and deciphering the third language, which was used to write the middle text of the stone, in the first decade of the 20th century the thesis that three scripts and two languages were used on the stone began to predominate. Consequently, current scholarship supports the theory that two scripts: the hieroglyphic and the demotic, were used to inscribe the decree on the Rosetta Stone in ancient Egyptian language.

A basic assumption of our research is that in writing the text on the Rosetta Stone three scripts were used, but in three languages: ancient Egyptian written in the hieroglyphic script, ancient Macedonian written in the 'demotic script', and ancient Greek written in the ancient Greek alphabet. This assumption is based on the fact that the rulers of Egypt in those times were the Ptolemaic dynasty, descend from Ptolemy Soter, general of Alexander the Great, i.e. they were ancient Macedonians. And according to the perceptions of a part of contemporary scholarship the ancient Macedonians used to speak in a language different from the ancient Greek, and it is more than obvious that they had to know how to read and write into their own language. Our assumption is that the script they used was the script used in the middle text of the Rosetta Stone, and which is known today in the scholarly circles under the term of the 'demotic script'. The assumption becomes true if the demotic script is taken into consideration either in its universal use on the part of the literate people of those times, i.e. it was being used in Persia and Egypt for writing state documents, documents for legal and property issues, scientific texts, poetry and prose."

This painstaking work involved in translating the script by these two great men, Tome and Aristotel, fascinated the academic world as there were countless examples of this ancient script, very similar to that of the modern Macedonian language and it suddenly all began to make sense.

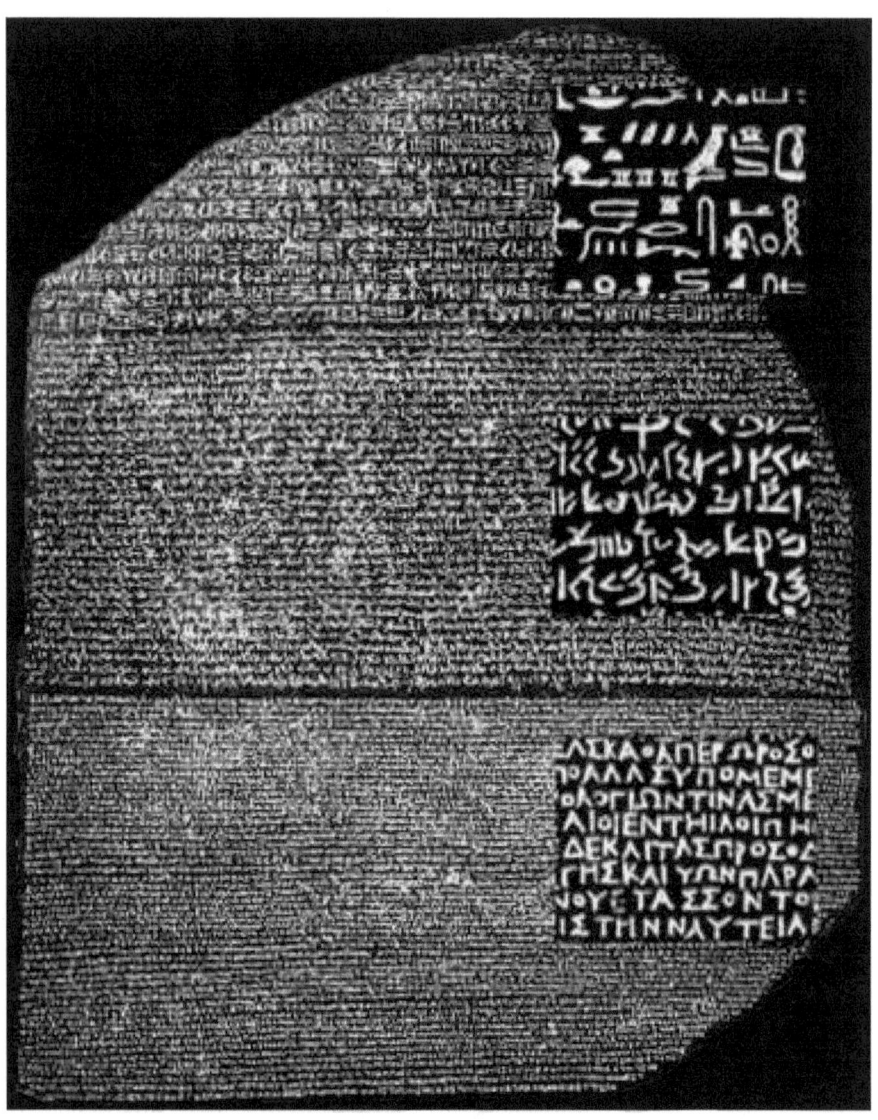

ROSETTA STONE – THE MONUMENT OF SCRIPT AND LANGUAGE

Tome Boshevski, MASA
Aristotel Tentov, FEEIT

- Introduction
    - Basic characteristics of the script
    - Identified signs
    - Algorithm for wiring for sound
    - Few grammatical rules
    - Transliteration and English translation of rows 22 to 32
    - Our readings and archeological evidences
    - Naming the gods in the different languages
    - Naming the different nations and citizens of towns
    - Different way of communication with different nations
    - Analysis of the last three orders in the demotic text
    - Examples of texts on artifacts from Macedonia and Vincha
- Conclusion

	Signs with the same form and sound				
Number	Cyrillic/Latin alphabet	Ancient Macedonian script	Number	Cyrillic/Latin alphabet	Ancient Macedonian script
1.	J	J	8.	I	I
2.	P	P	9.	O	⊗
3.	Д	Л	10.	У	⊥
4.	Ђ	ʃ			
5.	Л	λ			
6.	V	⋁			
7.	E	*E*			

EINE VERLORENE SPRACHE

Der Schlüssel zur Entzifferung der Hieroglyphen ist ein Stück schwarzen Basalts, das während Napoleons ägyptischer Kampagne im Jahre 1799 von französischen Soldaten, die in der Nähe von Rashid oder Rosette schanzten, gefunden wurde. Die Inschrift, die auf ihnen enthalten ist – ein Loblied auf Ptolemäus V. aus dem Jahre 196 v. Chr. –, ist von geringer Bedeutung. Unschätzbar aber ist die Tatsache, daß der Text nämlich in zwei Sprachen eingemeißelt ist: in Griechisch und in einer spätägyptischen Schrift, die demotisch genannt wird. Obwohl die Gelehrten die außerordentliche, geradezu sensationelle Wichtigkeit dieses Fundes sofort erkannten, dauerte es noch 23 Jahre, ehe das „Stein von Rosette" sein Geheimnis durch die Entzifferung eines einzigen Wortes (pyramiden) preisgab.

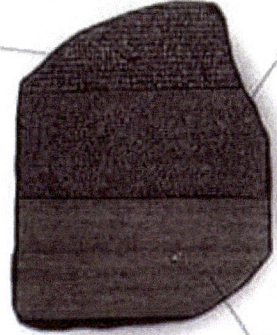

Der Stein von Rosette, 1799 von J.-F. Champollion, einem Offizier der napoleonischen Armee in Ägypten gefunden, war der Schlüssel zur Entzifferung der ägyptischen Hieroglyphen. Derselbe Text findet sich in drei verschiedenen Schriften darauf: in Hieroglyphen sowie in Altmakedonisch und in Makedonische Koine Zeichen. Rechts steht der Name Ptolemäus in allen drei Schriften. Seine Entzifferung war der erste Schritt zur Entzifferung der Hieroglyphen.

Hieroglyphen

Altmakedonisch

ΠΤΟΛΕΜΑΙΟΣ Makedonische Koine

Simon Tasievski

THE NAME DISPUTE

I honestly don't believe I could have worded this any better - I own multiple books and manuscripts written by the wonderful Risto Stefov and here he says it best. Below is an excerpt from his book on the name dispute with very small parts added or amended by me – but the vast majority is all him:

Risto Stefov: *"The Name Game: Greece's Objections to Macedonia's Name"* 2014

"As much as I want to get away from discussing the so-called "name dispute" between Greece and Macedonia I am again drawn into it by "the Macedonian preoccupation" with this Greek-invented issue.

First let me say that there is no "name dispute" between Greece and Macedonia. The name "Macedonia" belongs to the Macedonian people and there is no question about that. The problem here is that Greece has "invented" the so-called "name dispute" to divert attention from some "other issues" that it doesn´t want known.

Second, let me say that to this day I have not heard Macedonia complain about Greece using the name "Macedonia". So where is the "name dispute"?

Greece claims that the name "Macedonia" is exclusively Greek and no one except Greece has a right to use it. If that were true then why hasn´t Greece complained about any other countries, Australia for example with the Macedon ranges or the USA using the name "Macedonia" for several of its towns?

What Greece *actually* means is that "it doesn´t want the country Macedonia" to use this name. But if anyone has any right to use this name then, for obvious reasons, it should be Macedonia the country.

Aside from the fact that the name Macedonia was never Greek, not in prehistoric, not in ancient, not in medieval and not in modern times, then how does Greece justify the name "Macedonia" being Greek? Well in this case Greece doesn´t have to justify anything; it only has to "declare" because that is how Greece has been operating over the last two centuries - unchallenged.

You see Greece has been allowed to get away with all sorts of things like declaring (not justifying or proving) that Greece is a homogeneous nation, and that all Greeks are descendants of the ancient Greeks. In this regard Greece has been allowed to push the envelope to the limit, bordering on the bizarre, without ever been asked to explain itself or to justify these claims. So, if Greece can claim it is a homogeneous nation of pure Greeks, descendants of the ancient Greeks, without once being challenged, then why not declare that the word "Macedonia" is Greek and only Greek? Who is going to dispute that? And that is exactly what they did.

Can Greece answer why the name "Macedonia" became "exclusively" Greek only *after* it discovered that the Republic of Macedonia was about to declare its independence from the Yugoslav Federation in 1991? Why didn´t Greece voice concerns in 1945 when the Republic of Macedonia became a Republic in the Yugoslav Federation by using exactly that very same name. Why the concern now?
Was it by any chance that when the Republic of Macedonia declared its independence from the Yugoslav Federation,

Greece was caught by surprise and didn't know what else to do so it invented the name issue?

Greece, for almost a century, has been struggling to smother the Macedonian identity living on its own soil since Greece illegally invaded, occupied, and annexed Macedonian lands. Then all of a sudden, an entire nation of Macedonians gained their independence just next door. Panic stricken and not knowing what to do, Greece invented a problem in hopes of putting the Macedonians on the defensive.

What if these Macedonians started to expose how their compatriots in Greece were treated over the years? What if those who were wronged, exiled, had their citizenship taken away, had their lands and properties confiscated, families and relatives jailed, abused, and murdered, what if they started speaking up about it all? Well, they certainly can't have the world know about any of that! After all, we're in modern times now and the news travels much faster across the world than it did in the past!

So, what to do? Why not then "invent" a problem for the Macedonians to focus on; like they can't have the name "Macedonia" because that name is exclusively Greek?

If Greece suddenly assumed the victim role and without being provoked declared, (as it is used to falsely declaring), that "big bad Macedonia" wants to usurp their so-called "Greek name" because this nation of bad people has "territorial aspirations" towards its own non-existent northern province also called "Macedonia", then perhaps it could get some attention. Perhaps if it screamed "rape and murder" long and loud enough then someone might hear and come to its rescue.

Greece could only have done this in panic mode and without thinking because it doesn't take a genius to figure out that (1) Greece acquired these territories that it calls its "northern province of Macedonia", which by the way did not exist as a province, illegally and by war and conquest which is factually proven by the very existence of the Treaty of Bucharest, and (2) that these Macedonian territories never at any time belonged to Greece. Macedonia never belonged to the so-called ancient Greeks and has never belonged to the artificially created modern Greeks.

Greece has successfully created a "distraction" for the Macedonian people, particularly for the Macedonian authorities, leading them to focus on non-issues like the so-called "name dispute" instead of focusing on the real problems that the Macedonian people have with Greece, that Greece is desperately trying to avoid and to cover-up.
And what may these problems be?

Well for starters, not having recognized the Macedonian minority living inside Greece. Greece does not want to recognize a Macedonian minority because Greece's aim all along has been to "eradicate" the Macedonian identity. Why would Greece want to recognize a people which, for more than a century, it has been bent on eradicating?

In its attempt to extinguish the Macedonian identity, Greece has illegally expropriated Macedonian lands and committed many atrocities against the Macedonian people. Greece, for example, has been exiling citizens because they were Macedonians and for years has been expropriating their properties and lands without any compensation. Just deciding they will take it for the state.

So where does Greece stand with regard to the Macedonians?

One can't trust what Greece says, one has to observe what Greece does and how it behaves around the Macedonian issue in order to understand what is really going on. Who is better qualified to give you any insight into Greece regarding the Macedonian questions than the Macedonians who, as Macedonians, have lived and experienced it within Greece themselves firsthand?

There is no doubt in my mind that Greece's aim is to eradicate the Macedonian existence once and for all, albeit unsuccessfully. I base this fact on Greece's historic treatment of the Macedonians. It is not that Macedonians don't exist - it is Greece's adamant wish that Macedonians do not exist that gives away its attitude towards them and its long-term aim to eradicate them.

Since it conceived the idea of "acquiring Macedonian lands", Greece has been fanatical in its aim to deny the Macedonian existence. That fanatical attitude has not changed since it acquired Macedonian lands to this very day. Today as Macedonians are recognized worldwide, Greece still aggressively maintains that they don't exist. This is why I have no doubt that Greece's behaviour has nothing to do with the "name" and everything to do with the Macedonian identity. If Greece succeeds in removing the name from the Macedonian people, it will be its first step in removing the Macedonian identity, as well as all the atrocities it did to those people.

Again, I will reiterate that there is no doubt in my mind that Greece is out to permanently destroy the Macedonian identity not only inside Greece but everywhere, including inside the Republic of Macedonia.

And now to discuss the reason why I was drawn into this embroilment.

Every Macedonian by now should have realized that Greece doesn't care about the name "Macedonia". It never did since 1913 when it acquired Macedonian lands right up until 1991 when the Republic of Macedonia declared its independence. Also, if the Macedonians had been paying attention, they would have easily discovered Greece's real aim, which is to eradicate everything that is Macedonian; the name, the language, the ethnic identity, absolutely everything. Just as it had destroyed everything Macedonian inside Greece by denying the Macedonian existence, by changing peoples' names, by renaming place names, by erasing Macedonian writing, by destroying Macedonian monuments, by rewriting the names on tombstones of the dead to Greek sounding names.

Greece is now attempting to do the same thing but this time outside of Greece. By banning the Macedonian language, by assimilating the Macedonian population into the Greek fold and by exiling, torturing and murdering the non-conformists, Greece has amply proven its hatred for the Macedonian people both inside and outside its own borders.

Every Macedonian by now should know that Greece does not want our name. It is bent on destroying Macedonians to the last one. Greece could have used the name Macedonia since 1913 but those who experienced life in Greece know first-hand about Greece's hatred for that name and everything it represents including banning the word from even being spoken. For almost a century Greece has desperately tried to bury that name in the darkness of hell. What would make anyone now think that "Greece is suddenly in love with that particular name?"

If it is clearly understood where Greece stands with regard to the Macedonian issue, it makes me wonder why there are so many Macedonians still preoccupied with the "name game" when they know very well that (1) Greece is not after the name. The name is only a ploy, a ruse to distract them from focusing on real issues, and (2) why are they negotiating something they know (a) Greece does not want and (b) the Macedonians cannot and will not give up?

What is the point of "negotiating" something we can't possibly "sell", "trade", or "give away"?

Don't we know how this appears to the outside world? Negotiating our name!?

A name that has existed for over 3,000 years; a name passed on to us by countless generations. A name that is not ours to "negotiate", bargain with, sell, or give away. What are we thinking? If we continue to think this way of ourselves, what do we expect others to think of us? Have we paused for a moment, taken a deep breath, and seriously thought about this? The very idea of even thinking such a thought is completely insane wouldn't you agree?

Why do I think the "name" issue is a ruse to distract the Macedonian people from real issues?

Because the Macedonians, particularly those in charge, have been blinded and deafened by this "name dispute" and forgotten the real issues like:

1. The name "Macedonia" is autochthonous and belongs to the region and to those who lived in that region the longest. Only they have the right to call themselves "ethnic Macedonians"; not the recent settlers, invaders and conquerors who acquired it by force of arms.

2. Macedonia belongs to the Macedonian people. It is the property of those who live on it, own lands on it and pay taxes. It is not the property of the overlords who from time to time occupy it by force. Greece invaded, occupied, and annexed those lands in 1912, 1913 illegally just as the Ottomans did 500 years earlier. So, if after 500 years the Ottomans were considered "occupiers" then that is exactly how the Greeks should also be considered.

3. On those Macedonian lands that Greece occupies today there live Macedonians who are neither acknowledged nor have any human rights. As I said earlier, their names were forcibly changed, and their language banned. This is a real issue that Macedonian authorities should be negotiating with Greece. Forget I said "negotiating"; this is an issue that Macedonian authorities should be screaming about to the world.

4. There are over 28,000 refugee children, now elderly men and women with families of their own, who were exiled by Greece in 1948 during the Greek Civil War and who are still not allowed to return to Greece because they are Macedonians. This is another "real" issue about which Macedonian authorities should be screaming to the world.

5. Since Greece illegally acquired Macedonian territories, it has been exiling Macedonians and illegally confiscating their properties without compensation. This is not only immoral, but also illegal.

By international law, no one has the right to confiscate peoples' properties without compensation. This is yet another "real" issue that Macedonian authorities should be publicly pursuing.

6. Since the 1920's Greece has been "Hellenizing" Macedonia by destroying what was real Macedonian and replacing it with "artificial Greek". The reason I call it "artificial" is because prior to the Greek occupation, be it a person's name or toponym, it never existed by that name (the modern one). I have thousands of examples of this, but I will demonstrate it with a single example. Up until the early 1920's, a village with a long history and tradition, was called "Oshchima". The Greeks renamed it "Trigonon". Oshchima, along with its long history and traditions, died when it was renamed; when it was given an alien, meaningless foreign name, a name to remind the people of Oshchima that they were now captives of a foreign overlord who neither had the decency nor the humanity to allow us to be who we are! My wish, and the wish of so many thousands of Macedonians who lived and still live in Greece is to see our own Macedonian language and Macedonian names reinstated; be it personal names or place names. This is a human rights issue that concerns thousands of Macedonians, a "real" issue that Macedonian authorities should be publicly pursuing.

7. The next time Greece claims, "the name Macedonia is Greek" Macedonian authorities should be challenging that claim by asking for proof. (1) To which "Greeks" did that name and land belong? (2) How did these so-called "Greeks" acquire that name and land? (3) When did these so-called "Greeks" acquire the name and land? And (4) what do the artificial modern Greeks have to do with it? If the modern Greeks have the audacity to deny the existence of the Macedonian identity, surely Macedonians have not only the right to question the validity of

these "Greek" claims but also the right to challenge the Greeks about their own identity.

8. The real bargaining chip Macedonian authorities have over Greece is what Greece fears the most; losing Macedonia to the Macedonian people (or should I say "giving Macedonia back to the Macedonian people"). Greece has a primordial physiological fear over this, and it shows. In spite of the reassurances that the entire world gave Greece and despite the fact that the Macedonian national flag and constitution were amended by the Republic of Macedonia, Greece still fears the Republic of Macedonia having "territorial aspirations" towards its so-called northern province also called "Macedonia". This guilt and anxiety can truly be exploited. Greece is not afraid of Macedonia or of the Macedonian people over this. Greece is afraid that some Great Power, like Australia or the United States, might someday listen to the pleas of the Macedonian people and come to their rescue. I am sure more than any other country, the United States would love to see Greece parceled up into small pieces and Greece is well aware of this.

Wasn't it Henry Kissinger who said, "get rid of Greece if you want peace in the Balkans"? I am not suggesting here that Macedonian go to war over this, because this is the only way Greece would give up the Macedonian territory it occupies, but I am suggesting that it is something that Macedonians can "negotiate" with Greece. For example, Macedonia can keep this issue to itself, for now, if Greece abstains from vetoing its entry into international institutions, like the United Nations, under its constitutional name.

9. Speaking of entering the United Nations by its constitutional name, why "negotiate" with Greece over a non-issue when Macedonian authorities could go directly to the United Nations

and challenge the legality of their entry as Dr. Igor Janev has suggested over a thousand times? Why not withdraw from the UN and re-apply with the name "Republic of Macedonia" and see what happens?

10. When the Macedonian authorities entered into "negotiation" with Greece they legitimized the non-issue and made it into an actual issue. If something is mine, then it is mine and only mine; not yours or ours. When I begin "negotiating" over something that is clearly mine then I give the impression that it "is not really mine" and give legitimacy to the other person´s claim. This is what Macedonian authorities have done with our name and this is how it is viewed from the outside world despite the pleas and objections from the Macedonian people.

The "dignified" way to end this is by admitting that "we did not know what we were getting into" before we got into the "negotiating" process with Greece and to bow out of it once and for all.

That which we inherited is not ours to squander because if we do, we will be known as the generation of "greatest traitors" in Macedonian history who "willingly" sold out our inheritance; an inheritance for which our forefathers spilled blood to pass onto us and we did this willingly and voluntarily with our eyes and ears open."

Macedonia: A History

Simon Tasievski

BIBLICAL REFERENCES TO MACEDONIA

As was mentioned at the beginning of this book, there are over 27 direct references to Macedonia as a country in the Holy Bible and many more indirectly. It was never referred to as a city because a city called Macedonia doesn't, and did not exist, now or then.

Greece, Bulgaria, Serbia, and Albania are never mentioned because they simply weren't even countries 2,000+ years ago when the Holy Bible was written.

What the Jews in ancient times called "Greeks", meant for any non-Jew living north of the Mediterranean Sea anywhere from Europe. Everyone and anyone from the continent of Europe was called a Greek. For those non-Jews in the Middle East - they were called and referred to as Gentiles.

Macedonia: A History

BIBLICAL REFERENCES:

And a vision appeared to Paul in the night; There stood a man of Macedonia, and prayed him, saying, Come over into Macedonia, and help us. And after he had seen the vision, immediately we endeavoured to go into Macedonia, assuredly gathering that the Lord had called us for to preach the gospel unto them. Therefore, loosing from Troas, we came with a straight course to Samothracia, and the next day to Neapolis; And from thence to Philippi, which is the chief city of that part of Macedonia, and a colony: and we were in that city abiding certain days. And on the sabbath we went out of the city by a river side, where prayer was wont to be made; and we sat down, and spake unto the women which resorted thither. And a certain woman named Lydia, a seller of purple, of the city of Thyatira, which worshipped God, heard us: whose heart the Lord opened, that she attended unto the things which were spoken of Paul. And when she was baptized, and her household, she besought us, saying, If ye have judged me to be faithful to the Lord, come into my house, and abide there. And she constrained us. And it came to pass, as we went to prayer, a certain damsel possessed with a spirit of divination met us, which brought her masters much gain by soothsaying: The same followed Paul and us, and cried, saying, These men are the servants of the most high God, which shew unto us the way of salvation.

Acts 16:9-17 KJV

Now when they had passed through Amphipolis and Apollonia, they came to Thessalonica, where was a synagogue of the Jews: These were more noble than those in Thessalonica, in that they received the word with all readiness of mind, and searched the scriptures daily, whether those things were so. But when the Jews of Thessalonica had knowledge that the word of God was preached of Paul at Berea, they came thither also, and stirred up the people. And then immediately the brethren sent away Paul to go as it were to the sea: but Silas and Timothy abode there still. And they that conducted Paul brought him unto Athens: and receiving a commandment unto Silas and Timothy for to come to him with all speed, they departed.

Acts 17:1, 11-11, 13-15 KJV

And when Silas and Timothy were come from Macedonia, Paul was pressed in the spirit, and testified to the Jews that Jesus was Christ.

Acts 18:5 KJV

After these things were ended, Paul purposed in the spirit, when he had passed through Macedonia and Achaia, to go to Jerusalem, saying, After I have been there, I must also see Rome. So he sent into Macedonia two of them that ministered unto him, Timothy and Erastus; but he himself stayed in Asia for a season. And the whole city was filled with confusion: and having caught Gaius and Aristarchus, men of Macedonia, Paul's companions in travel, they rushed with one accord into the theatre.

Acts 19:21-22, 29 KJV

And after the uproar was ceased, Paul called unto him the disciples, and embraced them, and departed for to go into Macedonia. And when he had gone over those parts, and had given them much exhortation, he came into Greece, And there abode three months. And when the Jews laid wait for him, as he was about to sail into Syria, he purposed to return through Macedonia.

Acts 20:1-3 KJV

And entering into a ship of Adramyttium, we launched, meaning to sail by the coasts of Asia; one Aristarchus, a Macedonian of Thessalonica, being with us.

Acts 27:2 KJV

"For it hath pleased them of Macedonia and Achaia to make a certain contribution for the poor saints which are at Jerusalem."

Romans 15:26 KJV

"It hath pleased them verily; and their debtors they are. For if the Gentiles have been made partakers of their spiritual things, their duty is also to minister unto them in carnal things."

Romans 15:27 KJV

"Now I will come unto you, when I shall pass through Macedonia: for I do pass through Macedonia."

1 Corinthians 16:5 KJV

"And to pass by you into Macedonia, and to come again out of Macedonia unto you, and of you to be brought on my way toward Judaea."

2 Corinthians 1:16 KJV

"Furthermore, when I came to Troas to preach Christ's gospel, and a door was opened unto me of the Lord, I had no rest in my spirit, because I found not Titus my brother: but taking my leave of them, I went from thence into Macedonia."

2 Corinthians 2:12-13 KJV

"For, when we were come into Macedonia, our flesh had no rest, but we were troubled on every side; without were fightings, within were fears."

2 Corinthians 7:5 KJV

"Moreover, brethren, we do you to wit of the grace of God bestowed on the churches of Macedonia;"

2 Corinthians 8:1 KJV

"For I know the forwardness of your mind, for which I boast of you to them of Macedonia, that Achaia was ready a year ago; and your zeal hath provoked very many. Yet have I sent the brethren, lest our boasting of you should be in vain in this behalf; that, as I said, ye may be ready: Lest haply if they of Macedonia come with me, and find you unprepared, we (that we say not, ye) should be ashamed in this same confident boasting."

2 Corinthians 9:2-4 KJV

"And when I was present with you, and wanted, I was chargeable to no man: for that which was lacking to me the brethren which came from Macedonia supplied: and in all things I have kept myself from being burdensome unto you, and so will I keep myself. As the truth of Christ is in me, no man shall stop me of this boasting in the regions of Achaia."

2 Corinthians 11:9-10 KJV

"Now ye Philippians know also, that in the beginning of the gospel, when I departed from Macedonia, no church communicated with me as concerning giving and receiving, but ye only. For even in Thessalonica ye sent once and again unto my necessity."

Philippians 4:15-16 KJV

"So that ye were ensamples to all that believe in Macedonia and Achaia. For from you sounded out the word of the Lord not only in Macedonia and Achaia, but also in every place your faith to God-ward is spread abroad; so that we need not to speak any thing. For they themselves shew of us what manner of entering in we had unto you, and how ye turned to God from idols to serve the living and true God;"

1 Thessalonians 1:7-9 KJV

"And indeed ye do it toward all the brethren which are in all Macedonia: but we beseech you, brethren, that ye increase more and more;"

1 Thessalonians 4:10 KJV

"As I besought thee to abide still at Ephesus, when I went into Macedonia, that thou mightest charge some that they teach no other doctrine,"

1 Timothy 1:3 KJV

"This know also, that in the last days perilous times shall come. For men shall be lovers of their own selves, covetous, boasters, proud, blasphemers, disobedient to parents, unthankful, unholy, Without natural affection, trucebreakers, false accusers, incontinent, fierce, despisers of those that are good, Traitors, heady, highminded, lovers of pleasures more than lovers of God; Having a form of godliness, but denying the power thereof: from such turn away. For of this sort are they which creep into houses, and lead captive silly women laden with sins, led away with divers lusts, Ever learning, and never able to come to the knowledge of the truth."

2 Timothy 3:1-7 KJV

Simon Tasievski

NEWSPAPER ARTICLES REFERRING TO MACEDONIA 1814 – 1947 AND BEYOND

1814 - January 12: "The Serai stands in an open space, near the south-east corner of the Castron: it is a vast irregular pile of building. The great hall of this building was crowded with attendants of every variety in costumes, from red-shawled Macedonians and turbaned Osmanli, to the Albanian with his shaggy white capote, and the Greek archon in robes of ermine and enormous calpac." *("Travels in Sicily Greece and Albania"* by Rev. Thos. Smart Hughes, 1820, page 472).

1849 – Paparrigopoulos *'Textbook of General History'*: 'the Macedonian nation accomplished in the general history [of civilization] a different mission from that of the Hellenic nation' (Paparrigopoulos 1849-53, 1.193)'

1858 - English-Arabic dictionary: "Saklabah, The Sclavonians, supposed by the Arabians to be descended from Seclab, a son of Japhet. Under this name, however, the Mahometans comprehend often the Servians, Bulgarians, Moesians, Thracians, Albanians, Macedonians, and the northern parts of Greece." *("An English Arabic Dictionary"* by Josiph Catafago, 1858, page 131)

1890 – July 19th Vienna, Austria, *New York Times: VIENNA, July 18.* – The Porte has already made choice of three prelates for the vacant Macedonian bishoprics. They are Monsignor Theodosius for Uskab, Monsignor Sinessius for Ochrida and

Monsignor Jusma for Kossovo. All three are Macedonians who have never lived in Bulgaria nor concerned themselves with politics. The principle semi-official journals of the Greek Government, that is the Palingenesis, the Nea Ephemeris, and the Acropolis, are warmly protesting against the appointment of Bulgarian bishops in Macedonia. They say these bishops cannot be tolerated by the side of the Greek bishops, as Macedonia is the very core of Hellenism, and the whole future of Greece depends on its being able someday to annex that province. It is said in diplomatic circles that these complaints are producing in Constantinople quite a contrary effect to that which the writers desire. The Austrian and German Ambassadors at Constantinople have communicated an identical note to the Porte, in which they complain of the capture by brigands of the two Austrian engineers, Messrs. Mejor and Gersen and request that stringent measures may be taken to protect foreigners employed on public works in Turkey from similar misadventures. Herr Mejor was released 24 hours after his capture in order that he might fetch 1,000 pounds of the ransom demanded and make arrangements for the payment of the rest. The money was given to him by the local agents of the railway contractors, but on arriving at the place where he was to meet the brigands, he found that the whole band had been scared away by the Turkish soldiers having begun a premature pursuit. The consequence of this blunder is that the brigands have now carried away Herr Gerson into the mountains." (*The New York Times, July 19, 1890*)

1895 - *"MACEDONIAN SUCCESS"* London, July 29. – The correspondent of the Chronicle at Constantinople says: The Macedonians, after a sharp conflict with the Turkish troops, have captured the town of Mendik, southwest of Nevrokop. The victors burned the telegraph station and the Turkish headquarters. The Vienna correspondent of the Chronicle says;

According to the statement of the Roumanian minister at Constantinople many of the insurgents arrested in Macedonia were found to be Russian officers. The Porte intends to send the documents found in their possession to the powers as proof that the Macedonian uprising is due to Russian agents and energy. The Chronicle also has an editorial on the above information which regards affairs in the Balkan land as menacing the peace of Europe. 'We see no way out of the trouble' the editorial says, 'except by summoning another congress, failing in which we may expect atrocities in Macedonia and Albania."
THE GALVESTON DAILY NEWS, MONDAY JULY 29, 1895".

1896 - July 29th Athens, Greece in the *New York Times*. "CHRISTIAN VILLAGES BURNED". Greece Notified that She Must Not Assist the Macedonians. LONDON. July 28. – The Daily News will to-morrow publish a dispatch from its Athens correspondent stating that the Mussulmans have burned twelve Christian villages in the province of Selino and Herakleon and desecrated many churches. The Standard will to-morrow publish a dispatch from its correspondent in Berlin saying that the powers have notified Greece that they will withdraw all support from her if she continues to patronize or assist the insurgents in Macedonia." (*New York Times, July 29, 1896*)

1897 - March 14th Constantinople *New York Times*: "MACEDONIANS AND TURKS FIGHT LONDON", March 13. – A dispatch from Constantinople states that fighting has occurred near Gravena between a number of Macedonian insurgents and a body of Turkish troops. Details of the fight are lacking."
(*New York Times, March 14, 1897*)

1897 – March 5th Athens, Greece *New York Times*: "GREECE READY FOR WAR". She will yield to no admonition from the powers. PARIS. March 4. – It is reported that the Government is making preparations to order the mobilization of the Mediterranean reserve squadron, which will be sent to the Levant, under command of admiral Humann. Le Jour publishes a dispatch from its correspondent at Athens containing a report of an interview with King George of Greece, in which his Majesty declares that Greece is ready for war with Turkey and would yield to no admonition from the powers. The King is reported to have added that the powers might blockade Greece, but in the interior they would be powerless. The Greeks, he said, were fully prepared to fight to the death, and the Macedonians were eager to revolt." (*New York Times, March 5, 1897*).

1897 – *New York Times*: "Mr. Gladstone and the Balkan Confederation. – The Byron Society, which is actively engaged in disseminating appeals in Greece and Bulgaria to help the cause of the Macedonians, has communicated to its agents a letter from Mr. Gladstone for distribution in the vernacular in South-Eastern Europe. The Society aims at inducing the Greek, Servian and Bulgarian governments to come to an early agreement in reference to the Macedonian question. The letter is as follows: - 'Hawarden Castle Jan. 19, 1897. Dear, Sir, the hopelessness of the Turkish Government should make me witness with delight its being swept out of the countries which it tortures. Next to the Ottoman Government nothing can be more deplorable and blameworthy than jealousies between Greek and Slav and plans by the states already existing for appropriating other territory. Why not Macedonia for the Macedonians as well as Bulgaria for the Bulgarians and Servia for the Servians? And if they are small and weak, let them bind themselves together for defence, so that they may not be scattered by others, either great or small, which would probably be the effect of their quarrelling among themselves. Your very faithful, W. E. Gladstone.'"
(*"New York Times", February 6th, 1897*).

1897 - April 23rd: "Every friend of Greece will hope that not only the Bulgarians but the Macedonians and the Albanians, will also demand a redress of their grievances and threaten to mobilize their troops unless the Sultan consents to their wishes. The friends of Greece would not be sorry if the Sultan should refuse to do what the Bulgarians and Macedonians and Albanians want and if there should be a vigorous attack upon the Turkish intruding army from the rear."
(*The Brooklyn Daily Eagle – Friday, April 23rd, 1897*)

1900 – *New York Times: To the Editor of the New York Times* – The writer read with much interest a letter in THE TIMES of to-day "Christians in Turkey relating to the Macedonian disturbances". It has been said that 'The worst Christian Government is better than the best Muslim Government', but Mr. Burman, the writer of the letter in question, apparently thinks Turkish rule good enough in its way or feels that international justice demands that Turkey in Europe be preserved at any price. He speaks of 'acts of retribution on the part of their (the Macedonians') Turkish masters.' As the Turks have long referred to the Christians in their dominions as 'dogs' the term is perhaps a very apt one.
K. C. Bataille, Orange N. J., August 11, 1900."

1901 – May 12th Constantinople *New York Times*: "Wholesale Execution of Macedonians". VIENNA, May 11. – A dispatch from Constantinople announces the wholesale shooting of revolutionary Macedonians, including women. Twenty-four persons were executed at Monastir, fourteen at Beria, eighteen at Lating, eighteen at Seres and twenty-nine at Uskab."
(*New York Times, May 12, 1901*)

1901 - *October 10th*: In several quarters it has been intimated that the abduction of Miss Stone, the American missionary, was a political as well as a financial proceeding. That is to say, the brigands acted in connection with or at the instigation of the Macedonian committee. Aforetime, abductions have been traced to the Macedonian committee and while there is no positive proof that the organization was connected with the kidnappers of Miss Stone, it is possible such was the case..." (*Richmond Dispatcher, Thursday October 10th, 1901*)

1902 - *March 22nd New York Times*: "SERIOUS REVOLT IN ALBANIA" Rebels said to be masters of town of Yanina – fighting between Turkish troops and Macedonians. LONDON, March 22. – According to the Rome correspondent of the Daily Mail, the Italian consul at Yanina, southern Albania, has sent news of a serious revolution in Albania. The governor's palace at Yanina was attacked and several gendarmes were killed. The revolutionaries are masters of the town. The consul says further outbreaks have occurred at Berat, Paramythia and Avlona and that the revolution is spreading throughout Albania. The correspondent of The Morning Leader in Vienna reports a conflict between Turkish troops and Macedonian revolutionists at Sistova near Kastoria. The Turks surrounded the village and overcame the rebels. In the course of the fighting four Macedonians and two Turks were killed and twenty-six of the rebels were wounded. All the male inhabitants of the village were arrested. (*The New York Times, March 22, 1902*)

1902 – *March 31st Athens, Greece New York Times*: "*GREEKS BETRAY MACEDONIANS*". *Threatened Outbreak This Spring Will Probably Be Prevented – Montenegrins To Invade Turkey? London Times, New York Times Special Cablegram LONDON, March 31.* – A dispatch to The Times from Athens says the grave situation in Macedonia and Albania causes considerable uneasiness. It is thought that the propaganda from the Macedonian committee in Bulgaria is somewhat discredited among the wealthier classes, owing to the crimes and extortion connected with it. Still, the physical force party, which may be compared to the Fenian section of the Irish Nationalists, continues to follow the lead of President Sarafof who has planted a general rising of the Christians in the coming Spring. The dispatch says the overtures made in Athens and Belgrade have not been found tempting and that the Greeks have disclosed the scheme to Turkey. This, in conjunction with a strong military precaution being taken, will probably prevent the threatened outbreak. Improvement, however, is impossible without reform, and the Sultan's personal fears and the disunion of the European powers make the prospect of reform remote." (*The New York Times, March 31, 1902*)

1902 - *April 8th Vienna, Austria in the New York Times*: "MACEDONIANS WELL ORGANIZED". Have Even a Postal System of Their Own – They Have Received Donations from Abroad. London Times – New York Times Special Cablegram LONDON, April 8. – The Macedonian revolutionists are not concerned in regard to the convenience of Europe, says the Vienna correspondent of The Times. Sarafof (the Macedonian leader) deliberately says that it is beyond the power of Austria or Russia to interfere. The correspondent says that Sarafof's methods strongly resemble those of the anarchists, as they consist of terrorizing the defenseless population while the Turkish troops are carefully avoided. The revolutionists are admirable organized, having even an efficient postal service of their own. They have received donations from foreign sympathizers, and are likely to do more mischief before they are suppressed."
(*The New York Times, April 8, 1902*)

1902 - *Canadian Magazine of Politics, Science, Art and Literature*: "One thing that has to be remembered is that neither Macedonians nor Bulgarians are Greeks. They are mainly Slavs and will put up a stiff fight in the hilly country which will be the scene of operations if an uprising takes place." (*The Canadian Magazine of Politics, Science, Art, and Literature", Vol. XX, November 1902 to April 1903 inclusive, by John, A. Ewan, page 479*)

1903 – February 5th Salt Lake City, Utah: "IN THE BALKANS" It looks stormy in the direction of the Balkan states. Both Turkey and Roumania are purchasing large quantities of arms and ammunition, and Turkish troops are being massed along the Macedonian frontier. Austria-Hungary is said to have arranged for the mobilization of an eastern army corps, and the explanation that this is done in the interest of army maneuvers is not believed to be correct. The Macedonians claim that they have influential friends in Europe, who would come out for their cause if they had gained a victory or two over the Turks, and hence their plans for an early rising. It is also claimed that Russia and Austria have agreed on a scheme for the amelioration of the condition of the oppressed people of Macedonia, Albania, and Armenia. But as this plan involves practically autonomy, at least for the Macedonians and Albanians, it is believed that the Sultan will refuse to accede to any proposition of that kind. Those who have studied the situation believe that if the diplomats are unable to coerce Turkey and to prevent the contemplated rising in Macedonia, a great storm is likely to break out before long. The situation is interesting enough, for few doubt that such a storm must come before the millennial peace and calm can rest upon the surface of the earth." (*Deseret Evening News, Great Salt Lake City, Utah, February 6th, 1903, Last Edition*)

1903 – *Feb 16th Sofia, Bulgaria in New York Times*: "MASS MEETING OF MACEDONIANS" SOFIA, Feb. 15. – A mass meeting of 10,000 Macedonians was held here to-day to protest against the action of the government in dissolving the Macedonian Committees in Bulgaria. The meeting demanded the re-establishment of the Macedonian societies and the judicial punishment of individual offenders. It is reported that warrants are out for the arrest of Boris Sarafof, Yankof, and other Macedonian leaders. Sarafof is said to be now in Macedonia organizing a revolt. Several arrests of Macedonian leaders have been made in provincial towns. The government will prosecute the arrested men." (*The New York Times, February 16, 1903*)

1903 – *February 17th Sofia, Bulgaria New York Times*: "FEAR OF A BALKAN WAR". All the Powers working to bring about reforms peaceably. Chief Feature of Innovation is a Governor for Macedonia with Independent Powers – Bulgaria's good faith doubted. SOFIA, Bulgaria, Feb. 17. – The sobranje to-day, after a long and heated debate, adopted a resolution approving the action of the Government in suppressing the Macedonian committees. In the course of the discussions the Premier, Dr. Daneff, made an impassioned appeal to the house to support the Government, saying that it was imperative to the welfare of Bulgaria at the present critical moment that the powers should remain without any doubt as to the Bulgarian Government's intention to keep the people of Macedonia quiet and to help the powers in carrying out the scheme of pacification. VIENNA, Feb. 17. – The Neue Freie Presse announces that the Austro-Russian note was today submitted to the cabinets of Berlin, Paris, London, and Rome, and that it will be presented to the Porte on Feb. 19 unless the powers require a revision of it, in which case its presentation will be delayed until Feb. 21.
The reform proposals are chiefly of an administrative and financial nature, such as the Porte has heretofore promised but

never executed. One new feature is the appointment of a Governor, not necessarily a Christian, who shall have authority to act without referring to the Porte in every contingency. It is believed in diplomatic circles that the Porte will oppose the appointment of such a Governor, and it is seriously doubted whether the reforms will satisfy the Macedonians. The good faith of the Bulgarian Government in ordering the recent arrests of Macedonians is also questioned, in view of the fact that the most prominent revolutionists managed to escape.

A formidable outbreak in the early Spring is considered as by no means impossible. According to advices from Salonica, the German, British and Italian military attaches arrived in the city today from Constantinople."

(*The New York Times, February 17, 1903*)

1903 - February 24th: While reporting from various capitals in Europe concerning the Macedonian muddle continues to be contradictory and confusing, it is becoming more and more evident that the only unknown factors in this problem are the Czar and the Kaiser. In the meantime, while speculation halts at the problem of an alliance between the Kaiser and the Czar on the Macedonian problem, the force of circumstance is steadily tending towards a point where they will be compelled to play their hands out. The Macedonians and the Bulgarians appear resolved to put an end to diplomacy in the closet and force an open recognition of their claims. The Sultan on the other hand, appears to be as ready for war, as any of them. He has a good army, well equipped, and is ready to fight without pay. He whipped the Greeks very easily and he believes he can whip the Bulgarians and the Macedonians with an equal facility. In that belief he is doubtless right, but the power that left Greece at his mercy will not be so indifferent toward Macedonia..."

(*The San Francisco Call, Tuesday February 24th, 1903*)

1903 – *March 2nd Geneva in New York Times*: "*SEVERE FIGHTING BETWEEN TURKS AND MACEDONIANS: Turks Repulsed With Heavy Loss Near Monastir – Sultan's Reform Order Regarded as a Trick*". *LONDON, March 2. – The Geneva correspondent of The Daily Chronicle telegraphs that news has been received there of an engagement between Turkish troops and bodies of Macedonians and Bulgarians near Monastir. The Turks suffered a repulse. After the fighting thirty-two dead and many wounded were found.*" (*The New York Times, March 2, 1903*)

1903 - *May 27th New York Times*: "*MACEDONIAN CHIEF'S DEATH*" *A Greek Spy Betrayed Deltcheff's Whereabouts to the Turks. London Times - New York Times Special Telegram. LONDON, May 26. Detailed report of the death of Deltcheff, the famous Macedonian chief, says the Sofia correspondent of the Times, shown that he accompanied a band under Voivoda and Kirtchovski, together with the poet Tavaroff, and entered the village of Banitza, near Seres, where his presence was betrayed to the Turks by a Greek spy. A large force surrounded the village, and all the members of the revolutionary band were killed after a long resistance. It is stated that the inhabitants of the village, to which the Turks set fire, were also killed. Deltcheff was thirty-two years old. He was a schoolmaster, and practically created the present Macedonian organization, which has ramifications in all parts of the country. The Vienna correspondent of the times says persecutions and arrests continue in the vilayete of Andreanople. Numbers of priests and schoolteachers have been taken into custody. Arms have been found in six villages. The male population has fled, and agricultural work is at standstill.*" (*The New York Times, May 26th, 1903*).

1903 - *August 11, New York Times: "CHRISTIANS IN TURKEY" To the Editor of the New York Times*:
The Writer read with much interest the letter in The Times of today relating to the Macedonian disturbances. It has been said that 'the worst Christian Government is better than the best Muslim Government,' but Mr. Berman, the writer of the letter in question, apparently thinks Turkish rule good enough in its way or feels international justice demands that Turkey in Europe be preserved at any price. He speaks of 'acts of retribution on the parts of their (the Macedonians') Turkish masters.' As the Turks have long referred to the Christians in their dominion as 'dogs' the term is perhaps a very apt one. We rid Cuba of Spanish rule because it was felt the conditions there had become unbearable and because we considered that our peace and safety rendered it imperative that we do so. If Russia and Austria pursued a like course in the Balkans they would have at least as good cause for their actions as, had we, though of course such a move on their part would stir up trouble among other interested powers. The Macedonians, a hardy race of farmers and laborers, do not ask independence, but autonomy – the right to rule themselves, to have a voice in their own government. In this age of self-government surely, they are but asking for their own. In every vilayet in European Turkey outside of Constantinople, except in Albania, the Christian population outnumbers the Mohammedan, yet the Christians exist in a land of their fathers simply on sufferance. If one of them approaches a circle in which there are Christians and Mohammedans, he must first address the latter, after which he may speak to his own people. Let those who think Turkey should be kept alive at any price ponder the history of Bosnia and Herzegovina since they have passed under Austrian control. Let them consider the conditions of those states today and compare it with any period during which the Crescent floated over them. This is not an appeal for those people simply because they are Christians, but

because they are men living under conditions that we believe are intolerable, without political rights or any political or economic future. It is not desirable that this plum fall to either Austria or Russia, but evidently it will do so eventually unless all civilization rises up in arms for a people that has lived in Turkey for ages and yet are not Turks, a people honest, frugal, industrious, but a race of strangers without a country, in the valleys and on the hillsides that they have tilled for centuries. E.C. BATAILLE. Orange, N. J., August 11, 1903." (The New York Times, August 11, 1903)

1903 – August 15th Sofia, Bulgaria New York Times: "WILL AID MACEDONIANS" Bulgarian Plan to Collect Funds for the Insurgents. Government may be asked to intervene – Premier Petroff tells of his inspection of the frontier. SOFIA, Bulgaria, Aug. 15. – An enthusiastic meeting of Macedonian sympathizers was held here this afternoon, at which resolutions were adopted in favor of agitating throughout the country in order to being pressure to bear upon the Bulgarian Government to intervene in Macedonia. A committee was appointed to collect money to aid the insurgents. Premier Petroff has just returned from a visit to the Macedonian frontier where it touches the District of Dubnitza and takes somewhat of an optimistic view of the situation in Macedonia. He believes the outbreak will be confined in the vilayet of Monastir, where the Turks probably will succeed in suppressing the insurrection. When interviewed today by a representative of the Associated Press he discussed the condition of affairs frankly and at length. Regarding the reports that Bulgaria was responsible for the outbreak, he pointed out that the center of the disturbed area at present was nearly two-hundred miles from the Bulgarian frontier and was separated from it by a country largely inhabited by Turks. Consequently, he said. It was foolish to say that the movement was aided by bands from Bulgaria, and that it was equally unreasonable to suggest that the arms of the insurgents came from Bulgaria. As a matter of fact, he said, the guns used by the insurgents were all of French manufacture, and most of them had been bought from Turkish officers and men who, receive no pay, had resorted to sale of their guns and ammunition to obtain money. The insurrection, he said, was entirely a national Macedonian movement organized by the Macedonian Internal Committee, which in itself was proof of the shocking condition of affairs due to the excesses of Turkish soldiers, who, on the pretext of searching for arms, entered Macedonian villages to plunder and destroy. The situation in the unhappy villages, he said, was rendered more desperate by the refusal of the Turks to permit the unemployed to leave in order to secure work elsewhere. This goaded the population to the most desperate measures. Premier Petroff declared that the Bulgarian Government was doing its most to maintain peace. 'Not only is the frontier guarded to prevent crossing of individual bands' he said 'but a rigid inspection also exists at interior points, and it is absolutely certain that no bands, large or small, are passing the frontier at this time. A few individuals may, of course, be crossing. Little excitement or enthusiasm is evident in Bulgaria now, but should the unexpected happen, and a massacre of Bulgarians occur, or should the movement assume alarming proportions, the population of Bulgaria would naturally become greatly excited, and while the Government is most anxious to maintain peace, it would, of course, be forced to consider Bulgarian population sentiment. Thus, a most critical situation might arise. It appears now, however, as if the movement would be confined, notwithstanding the reports of its extension.'

M. Petroff says that the Turks are pouring overwhelming forces into Monastir, and that they are sufficient not only to suppress the present rising but to destroy the entire revolutionary movement, unless the Powers intervene to prevent Turkey from taking rigorous measures. Upon the whole, the Premier believes

there is no immediate cause for alarm. On the contrary, he is of opinion that the situation will soon change for the better."
(*The New York Times, August 15, 1903*)

1903 - *August 25th*: "An alliance [between Turkey and Greece] such as this would prove more effective than anything else in checking the designs which Russia is credited with having on Constantinople, and would prove of such inestimable advantage to the 8,000,000 Greeks living in the Ottoman Empire, giving them a preferred position over Bulgars, Serbs, Roumanians, Macedonians and Armenians that they may be relied upon to use all their influence to promote the successful conclusion of the negotiations."
(*The Washington Times, Tuesday, August 25th, 1903*)

1903 – *August 26th*: "THE BALKAN INSURRECTION" It is therefore quite understandable that religious fanaticism and intolerance, combined with racial and political prejudices, could cause Turks, Macedonians, Greeks, Albanians, and other races comprising the population of the Balkans to turn and rend each other if their passions are not kept in check by a government wise enough and strong enough to hold them."
(*West Coast Times, Wednesday, August 26, 1903, page2*)

1903 - *Monday, September 21st*: "BESIEGED MELNIK'S GARRISON IS IN CRITICAL CONDITION" Handfuls of Turks continue to hold out against fifteen hundred Macedonian insurgents while reinforcements are hastening to prevent the capture of the town. Famous retreat whence comes news of the progress of the siege of Melnik by Macedonians, and the German ambassador to the court of the Turkish Sultan…"
(*The San Francisco Call, Monday, September 21st, 1903*)

1903 – October 14th Vienna, Austria New York Times: "MACEDONIANS NEAR THE SEA" London Times – New York Times Special Cablegram. London, Oct. 14. – The Times's Vienna correspondent says that according to Politsche Corespondenz the insurgents in Sunjak, Seres are rapidly nearing the southern seacoast at Kavala." (*The New York Times, October 14, 1903*)

1903 – October 21st London, New York Times: "PLANS OF MACEDONIANS". Correspondent comes into touch with the insurgent leader. London Times – New York Times – Special Cablegram. LONDON, Oct. 21. – After a long journey in the night a special correspondent of the Times in Macedonia has succeeded in getting into touch with the leader of the Macedonian Revolutionists.

He was informed that it was the intention of the insurgents to carry on their guerrilla operations throughout the Winter so far as the climatic conditions will permit, in order to compel Turkey to keep a large army of pacification constantly under arms. The bands intend to make another desperate campaign in the Spring. The sole hope of the revolutionary leaders is to prolong the present disturbed state of affairs in order to prove to Europe that Turkey, in spite the enormous forces employed to suppress the insurrection, is unable to settle the Macedonian question. They feel confident that the powers will then force the Porte to grant the autonomy demanded by them. With regard to the atrocities perpetrated in Macedonia, the correspondent says, the insurgent leaders, who have no cause to love the Turks, do not endorse entirely the stories of vengeance perpetrated on innocent women and children that have been circulated by some hysterical correspondents. They say that the Turks massacre all male Macedonians suspected of sympathy with the insurrection and constantly fire on parties of refugees, but wholesale outrages on women and children have occurred only on occasions. The wholesale pillage and destruction of villages

and massacres of the males have been the method pursued by the Turks in dealing with the insurrection. The insurgent leaders have adopted a new policy in order to take from the Turks as far as possible any pretext for retribution of this sort. They have established food supplies in the mountains."
(*The New York Times, October 21, 1903*)

1903 – *November 7th Sofia, Bulgaria New York Times: "EMPEROR AIDS MACEDONIANS" Francis Joseph Gives 10,000f. for the Refuges in Response to an Appeal by Princes Clementine. London Times – New York Times Special Cablegram. LONDON, Nov. 7.* – The Sofia correspondent of the Times says Emperor Francis Joseph gives 10,000f. in aid of the Macedonian refugees. The donation was in response to an appeal by Princes Clementine of Belgium (Countess Lonyay, who was the wife of the Crown Prince Rudolf) and was accompanied by an autographed letter. The munificence of the Emperor is much appreciated in Sofia. The princess, who has been deeply touched by the sufferings of the unfortunate exiles, has addressed letters to several of her august relatives invoking aid and has contributed large sums from her private purse."
(*The New York Times, November 7, 1903*)

1903 – *December 3rd New York Times: "MACEDONIA'S HEROIC STRUGGLE FOR FREEDOM"* System of Operation Adopted by the Revolutionary Bands. Turkish soldiers fear them and avoid engagements – Women fighters as brave as the men. The insurgent bands in Macedonia are in organization and method of operation developed from the system used in Bulgaria before Bulgaria became free. At that time the bands were formed in Roumania and used Roumania as their base. The traditions of the leaders of these old Bulgarian bands are celebrated in song and story, and many of the chiefs after Bulgaria became free occupied important posts in the administration of the new country. The life of an insurgent is the greatest of hardship. He often goes days without food, seldom spends the night twice in the same place, and, of course, is in perpetual danger. Before joining a band the insurgent takes oath never to surrender. The conduct and the membership of the bands are practically in the hands of young men. There are, however, several known women among them. The most celebrated is Ekaterina Arnaudova. She is said to be one of the best shots in the Balkans, and there are many stories of her prowess. There are also many former schoolmasters among the insurgents. While I was in Bulgaria a former schoolmaster and his fiancé were both killed while fighting with one of the bands. The Macedonians were nearly freed from the Turks at the end of the Russo-Turkish war in '78. Knowing this and seeing the great prosperity of their kinsmen in Bulgaria, they have never ceased their struggle to obtain the same position. The movement began to be particularly strong in the early part of nineties and received great impetus in 1895, owing to the interest that Prince Ferdinand then took in their affairs. At the time Bulgarian officers, Sarafoff, among the number, first seriously attempted to raise an insurrection. This, however, was easily stifled by the Turkish soldiers.

However, the revolutionary propaganda made great headway among the younger generations in Macedonia, who became greatly interested in the work for future freedom. Rifles were obtained and military exercises were started in the villages. But for some time, a central organization was not worked out, or rather there were several conflicting small organizations. In a few years, however, one current became dominant, the one having for leaders Delcheff (since killed), Grooyeff now chief of the Monastir staff; Gyorcho Petroff, and Tattarcheff, the foreign representative. They took for their motto the words of Gladstone 'Macedonia for the Macedonians'. They differentiated themselves from the Bulgarians and the

Macedonians living in Bulgaria, who formed the old committee with headquarters in Sofia. After some struggle the Bulgarian committee were obliged to take the secondary role of gathering money and representing the movement before Europe. At the same time the internal committee of the Macedonians had to contend with discordant elements, but finally came into entire control. It then began to perfect its organization and systematize the levying of taxes, finally monopolizing the cause of liberation of Macedonia. Meanwhile, the committee at Sofia, very moderate in tone, gradually losing its influence, and at last was obliged to give way to a new and more radical policy. Sarafoff took the lead and the committee assented to his policy of terroristic activity by the internal organization. But this, of course, soon made the official existence of the Sofia committee impossible. Sarafoff's course was too severe, and he was obliged to give up the Presidency. The power fell into the hands of Gen. Tsoncheff, whose movements were supposed to be inspired by Prince Ferdinand. Sarafoff went to Macedonia, where he had since taken an active part as leader of one of the bands. Gen. Tsoncheff began propaganda for an immediate revolution in Macedonia. That started a new and bitter strife not only between the internal committees and the Sofia committees, but among the insurgents themselves, and many of the most important influential leaders inside Macedonia fell into the hands of the Turks. Gen. Tsoncheff, however, decided to force the situation, and, although the results showed that the organization was not in shape to proceed on the best lines, it showed that the elements were too many and too powerful to be stopped after the movement had once got under way. Then the internal organization after some hesitation decided to cooperate with Tsoncheff, and he on the other hand agreed to acknowledge the leadership of the internal committee. The whole region of insurrection had already been divided into circuits, and the members of the internal committee who survived divided among themselves the leadership of these circuits. To preserve unity of operation they held monthly meetings where the whole movement was discussed, and the programme adopted by majority vote. Communication among the bands in action was also well established. Their headquarters in the mountains are practically inaccessible to Turkish troops and at the present time they are well equipped with arms and ammunition. The Turkish army holds the insurrection at great awe, and never seriously seek and engagement with them. The whole force of the Askar or regular Turkish soldiers, as well as the Bashi-Bazouks, or irregulars is thrown on the defenceless population of the villages. Something of the spirit which animates these people can be shown by the following incident, which occurred after I had left Bulgaria. In the same compartment with me was traveling a young man, possibly twenty-five or twenty-six years old. We engaged in conversation, and when he learned that I was interested in the Macedonian movement, he told his own story in the calmest kind of way. He said: 'I am a Macedonian engineer. My father, mother, two brothers and two sisters were killed by the Turkish soldiers, so that all there is for me left to do is to fight as long as I can stand up. I have seven wounds, which I have not had time to have attended to. One in my knee is very serious and bothers me a great deal. I am out of Macedonia to get cartridges and dynamite for the band, but I am anxious to get back and begin fighting again as soon as I can. I may have a chance to have a surgeon examine the wounds on my knee, but I have no time to give to it, - as I want to return to the fighting as soon as possible.' This is one story of countless that I heard when down there, but it is quite a typical one. The demands of the insurrectionists are, however, very moderate. They offer no programme, but say they will lay down their arms as soon as a method is found for protecting life and property in Macedonia. But it must be a real method, and no paper reform will answer. They are going to

keep right on fighting until this is obtained beyond all question.
CHARLES R. CRANE, Chicago, Dec. 3, 1903."
(*The New York Times, December 3, 1903)*

1905 - *September 14th:* "PLOTS DISCOVERED TO KILL MONARCHS" Assassinations Planned of Peter of Servia and Ferdinand of Bulgaria. Vienna, Sept. 13. – According to telegrams received from Belgrade, a plot has been discovered there and at Sofia to foment a general outbreak in the Balkans with a view of compelling the interference of the powers in the hope that Macedonian autonomy would be proclaimed. The alleged plot, the telegrams say, included an intention to assassinate King Peter of Servia, and Prince Ferdinand of Bulgaria. Those engaged in the plot in Sofia have been imprisoned. It is added that the recent attempt to assassinate the Sultan of Turkey in the courtyard of the mosque in Constantinople is supposed to have been the work of the same organization."
(*The San Francisco Call, Thursday, September 14th, 1905*)

1906 – *March 19th Belgrade, Serbia New York Times:* "600 MACEDONIANS COMING" *Emigrating to America – Atrocities Still Going on in Turkey.* BELGRADE, March 18. – Six hundred Macedonian emigrants left here to-day for the United States by way of Feume. All of them possessed sufficient funds to permit their entering into the United States. Although the Turkish Government reports the conditions of the Macedonian valyets to be 'tranquil', it appears that, after all the efforts of the powers and the elaborate measures taken by the foreign gendarmerie officers, the condition of the Christian population is very little better than it was two years ago. On Feb. 28 Bulgaria addressed a 'note verbale' to the Ottoman Commissariat, calling attention on the suffering inflicted on the Bulgarians in Salonika and Monastir Provinces by Greek bands and by Turkish officials and troops. The note gave details regarding a series of atrocities perpetrated by Greek bands in recent times, including numerous cases of assassinations, arson, and pillage. Among the instances cited was an attack on the village of Bernek, where nine men and one woman were killed, others wounded and five houses burned: the burning of the village of Poutouros, where two men and one woman were murdered and two children committed to the flames; the burning of the village of Tzernitchani, and the series of exploits by the famous Capitan Panayoti, including the plundering of the village of Iveeni, from which twelve of the principle inhabitants were carried away and subsequently put to death." (*New York Times, March 19, 1906*)

1907 - Pennsylvania Statistics Office: "Iron and Steel Supplement – Labor…Macedonians…17" (*"Annual Report of the Secretary of Internal Affairs of the Commonwealth of Pennsylvania", Part III, Industrial Statistics, Vol. XXXV, 1907, page 73*)

"Labor Supplements – Sole and Harness Leather…Macedonians…43" (*"Annual Report of the Secretary of Internal Affairs of the Commonwealth of Pennsylvania", Part III, Industrial Statistics, Vol. XXXV, 1907, page 191*)

"Labor Supplements – Tanning Extracts…Macedonians…3" (*"Annual Report of the Secretary of Internal Affairs of the Commonwealth of Pennsylvania", Part III, Industrial Statistics, Vol. XXXV, 1907, page 247*) Statistics office in 1907 to record 17 Macedonians working with iron and steel, 43 Macedonians working with sole and harness leather and 3 Macedonians working with tanning extracts.

1907 - *October 12th*: The state of affairs in the Balkans is not by any means reassuring, although the same might have been remarked any time within the last ten years, or even longer. Today's cable messages tell us that the Creusot works have at the present time a contract for the delivery during 1908 for material and ammunition for Servia, and that the same firm has also been entrusted with the manufacture of materials for new artillery for Greece. For some time now the Serbs, the Greeks, the Bulgars and the Macedonians have been annoying each other more than any occasion during a comparatively short period, and, as usual, it is very hard to form a just conclusion as to which is the most to blame." (*Evening Post, Volume LXXIV, issue 90, October 12, 1907, page 4*)

1908 - *January 20th Sofia, Bulgaria New York Times:* "OUTRAGE BY GREEKS". Macedonians Driven into Houses and Burned to Death. SOFIA, Bulgaria, Jan. 19. – News has reached here of a terrible tragedy at the village of Dragosch, near Monastir, a town in Macedonia, several days ago. While a festival was in progress and the villagers were dancing upon the lawns in the public park, a large band of Greeks suddenly swooped down upon them and after driving them into their houses, set fire to the buildings and burned them to death. The victims included women and children and numbered, it is said, between twenty-five and forty-five. (*The New York Times, January 20, 1908*)

1908 - *September 7th*: "OTTOMANS CELEBRATE". Letter from President. Rejoice over promulgation of Constitution in Turkey. Every seat and every foot of standing room in Carnegie Hall was occupied last night by a wildly enthusiastic audience of Ottoman subjects and sympathizers who met in mass meetings to celebrate the promulgation of the constitution in Turkey. The meeting was in joint auspices of the Young Turks, the Armenian Revolutionary Federation and the Hunchakist Society, and every

form of revolutionist from that part of the world represented by those people who were present, and a few more from Russia. There were Turks, Armenians, Macedonians, Syrians, Bulgarians, Albanians, and a few Greeks, while the Russian element consisted of Jewish Zionists and the revolutionists. The latter fastened their bright red standard on the gallery hall while the flags of the other elements were draped on the wall behind the stage, where also were hung a number of signs in different languages - some in English with inscriptions like these: "Liberty, Equality, Fraternity." Hurrah for the Young Turks and Armenian Revolutionary Federation." The speeches also were in general tongues, English, Turkish, Armenian, and Arabic."
(*New York Daily Tribute, Monday September 7th, 1908*)

1908 - December 31st: "1909 Four Celebrations of New Year's Day". New Year is celebrated in this country at least on four different dates in addition to the regular New Year's celebration on January 1st. With the Greeks, Russians, Servians, Bulgarians and Macedonians, all of whom adhere to the Greek Catholic Church, New Years is one of the most pleasant if not the pleasantest festival of the year. The Macedonians, Servians and Bulgarians celebrate the New Year, perhaps less elaborately, also on the same day as their Greek and Russian coreligionists."
(*The Winchester News, December 31st, 1908*)

1911 – Iowa: "FEW BOHEMIANS ARE COMING OVER FIND GOOD CHANCES IN NATIVE HEALTH SAYS REV. ZILKA." As I skimmed through the article my eye caught the following paragraph; "Rev. Zilka stated that the future immigrants to the United States will be coming from Russia and the Balkan states. They will be mostly Russians, Servians, Kroatians, Macedonians, Slovaks and Greeks." (*The Cedar Rapids Evening Gazette, Cedar Rapids, Iowa, Thursday, January 26, 1911, page 12*)

1911 - *September 23rd "THE PROBLEM OF TURKEY INEXPLICABLE MODE OF ACTION"* "The three might be added [to] the murders of Bulgarians, Macedonians, Greeks and Serbs who have been done to death with the old religious fury which is as prevalent as ever."
(*Evening Post, Issue 73, September 23rd, 1911, page 10*)

1912 – *November 22nd Athens, Greece: "GREEK ARMS FLORINA OCCUPIED AN AMBUSH". Received November 22, 10 a.m. Athens, 21st November.* The Greeks under the Crown Prince have occupied Florina (15 miles south-south-east of Monastir), intercepted the retreat of the Monastir army's rear guard. Greek, Bulgarian and Servian officers at Salonika are warmly fraternizing. Public fetes are being held. Eight hundred wounded have arrived here from Salonika. A Russian cruiser has hastily sailed for Jaffa in consequence of reported massacres of Christians. A band of Macedonians ambushed 500 Turkish regulars in the Janina district, killing twenty-four and wounding seventy-seven. The rest fled."
(*The Evening Post, Volume LXXXIV, Issue 125, November 22, 1912, page 7*)

1913 – *February 10th Winnipeg:* "The government has decided to expel all Greek journalists and is also causing the arrests of all Greeks, Bulgarians, and Macedonians, who will probably be sent out of the country."
(*Winnipeg Free Press, Monday, February 10, 1913*)

1913 - *August 19th:* "*The Macedonians Show Patriotism For Country All Over The World They Are Sore Over Balkan Affair Want War Continued Macedonians of United States Pass Resolutions Condemning Recent Balkan Treaty.* A new phase to the Balkan situation came to light today, through a local source, when it was learned that the Macedonians all over the world deeply resent the action which will be the result of the recent Balkan treaty. The Macedonians of America are leading a world-wide movement among the people of that race to rebel against the carrying out of the treaty, inasmuch as it means the elimination of Macedonia as a country and a world power. Under the treaty, Macedonia is now recognized except as a large amount of territory to be divided among the recent contestants. A large part of the country would fall under Grecian rule, and it is asserted that the Macedonians would even change their religion to escape from the rule of Greece. A set of resolutions have been prepared by a secret committee of Macedonians, representing that race in America, and similar resolutions have been passed by every Macedonian community throughout the world, according to an assertion from one of the Macedonians who is high up in the affairs of the local colony. A copy of the resolutions was received by the local colony today. 19 "The idea of adopting a new religion is spreading very rapidly among the Macedonians," said this man this morning. "The civilized world may be astonished to see that the entire Macedonian nation has thrown off the spiritual fetters by which the Greeks have held them for so many centuries." The Resolutions The set of resolutions were given to the News for publication, as it is said that they will be unanimously accepted by the members of the Macedonian colony of this city, as they have been by hundreds of other colonies in this and other countries. The resolutions demonstrate extreme patriotism and represent a world-wide movement. They are as follows: "As the representative of the Macedonian government, and having the authority to submit to the Macedonian government and the parliament a problem, in the solution of which your government ought to take part, we, the Macedonians of the United States of America, in our demonstrations and meetings, organized by the Macedonian Revolutionary Organization in the United States of America, on the 16th day of August, 1913, adopted and submit to your

government the following resolution-protest: "Whereas, The Balkan-Turkish war was declared and fought in the name of the freedom of Macedonia and the Christians in Turkey of Europe, in which war we, the Macedonians, fought most vigorously and with our help Turkey was defeated; "Whereas, The end of this Balkan-Turkish war was not the freedom of Macedonia, but most generous division of our country and people between Servia and Greece, and our nation was compelled to submit to the Servian and the Greek governments, a government more tyrannical than the Turkish government; and "Whereas, The Servian and the Greek governments now kill our fathers and our brothers, despoil the virtue and honor of our sisters, mothers and wives, and molest our children, all of which inhuman acts aim at the entire destruction of our national existence in Macedonia, and "Whereas, The present unjust division of our country was caused by the European diplomacy, and if the same exists in future there will always be internal revolutions and disturbances which will keep all the Balkan states in readiness for war and might throw all the European powers in disastrous clash; "Whereas, The peace in the Balkans is only the freedom based on the principle: 'Macedonia for the Macedonians.' "We, the Macedonians in the United States of America, with all the vigor in us, protest against the unjust division of Macedonia and the tyranny of the Servian and Greek governments in Macedonia; "We appeal to the European powers to declare the conference in Bucharest, Roumainia, between the representatives of the Balkan states unjust, and to demand autonomy of Macedonia; "We declare to all the nations of the world, that if the freedom of Macedonia is not granted soon, we will continue our struggle and fight for the freedom of our country, and we will all die or become free. We cry: 'Give us freedom or give us death.'" "The Committee for the Macedonians in U.S.A.""
(*The Fort Wayne Daily News, Tuesday, August 19th, 1913*).

1915 – *September 27th Rome, Italy: "Special Cable to The New York Times ROME, Sept. 27.* – Another great conflagration in the Balkans is unavoidable. Many Balkan exiles living in Italy, especially Greeks, Macedonians and Bulgarians are speeding home via Brindisi and Messina.
Another sign of the gravity of the situation is the fresh severity of the censorship in the Balkan countries practically allowing only the transmission of official news.
(*The New York Times, September 27, 1915*)

1915 - *"Special cable to the New York Times. Rome, Sept. 27.* – Another great conflagration in the Balkans is unavoidable. Many Balkan exiles living in Italy, especially Greeks, Macedonians, and Bulgarians are speeding home via Brindissi and Messina. Another sign of the gravity of the situation is the fresh severity of the censorship in the Balkan countries practically allowing only the transmission of official news."
(*The New York Times, September 27, 1915*)

1919 – *Cambridge Massachusetts: "A FREE MACEDONIA". A Government Like Switzerland's Being Urged Upon the Paris Conference By V.K. Sugareff. Cambridge, Mass., April 19, 1919.*
To the Editor of The New York Times: I beg your indulgence to insert a few remarks in the columns of your paper in connection with your editorial article of last Thursday's Times on "A Macedonian solution." Those of us, Macedonians, whose families have been scattered to the four winds as a result of the political unrest in the country, are quite convinced that the Macedonian question has not been presented to the American public in the light of an untainted justice. Should Macedonia be subjected to another pre-war régime, it will be a bitter disappointment to hundreds of us who donned the khaki to defend the honor of the United States and her broad principles which the Allies ultimately adopted. May I not, then, present

some gleanings which I have gathered at the feet of my professors here at Harvard, some of whom have gone to Paris to advise the President in these matters? The fact that nothing has been said publicly at the Peace Conference concerning the future fate of Macedonia is in itself a confession of the almost insurmountable difficulties involved in the so called "Macedonian Question." It is a question open to no dispute that an amicable solution of the Macedonian problem will be the only stable basis for a lasting peace in the Balkans. But how can the Macedonian question be settled so as to guarantee the future tranquility of the Balkans? Students of Balkan politics have suggested three methods for settling this all-important problem. The first method is repartition of Macedonia on the basis of the Bulgaro-Serbian treaty of 1912. While it provides the basis for negotiation between Bulgaria and Serbia, yet this method does not promise a favorable solution of the problem, for it opens no avenues for negotiation between Bulgaria and Greece, and between Bulgaria and Albania, the boundaries of which will certainly have to be rectified. The question of Thrace is also excluded from this treaty, and many other technical points will make a solution according to this method well-nigh an impossible undertaking. The second method provides that the principle of self-determination should be applied to Macedonia. This method is in accord with President Wilson's program, but few will doubt that the result will be overwhelmingly in favor of Bulgaria. Besides, it would have to be conducted under the supervision of the European powers in order to insure the people against an outside pressure which will certainly be used by the contending parties. In other words, there should be created in Macedonia such liberal conditions as exist in the United States to insure a successful execution of a plebiscite. But any one who has lived in Macedonia knows that it will take years to establish such favorable conditions under which a plebiscite can be successfully conducted. The third method, and the most acceptable to the Macedonians, is that Macedonia should be established as an independent State. The statement in The Times editorial article that in some quarters the Socialist Parties of the Balkan countries desire an independent Macedonia does not state the problem comprehensively. The European powers, the Balkan States, as well as the people themselves, have wanted to establish autonomy for Macedonia. Only a few precedents can be stated here. Had the organic law of 1866 been applied to Macedonia, as provided by Article 23 of the Berlin Treaty, Macedonia would have been an embryonic autonomous State. A European commission drew up in 1880 the so-called "Law of the Vilayets," which would have amounted to an autonomy for Macedonia had it been enforced. The Macedonian Revolutionary Committee, or otherwise known as the Central Committee, addressed to the Sultan Abdul Hamid in 1902 a memorandum in which the committee demanded autonomy for Macedonia, Albania, Old Serbia, and Adrianople. The Murzteg program of reforms, which was formulated by Austria and Russia, was in reality an official bluff to ameliorate the unbearable conditions in Macedonia, but it inspired the people with the hope of autonomy for Macedonia. Before the outbreak of the Balkan wars Austria and Russia advised an administrative decentralization of European Turkey. This would have established a self-government for Macedonia. The original memorandum of the Bulgaro-Serbian alliance in 1912 contained the following paragraph: "The renewal of the treaty of 1904, mutatis mutandis, instead of reform we shall ask for autonomy; if that should prove impossible we should divide Macedonia." Finally, it was virtually agreed between Bulgaria and Greece "to secure the respect of the privileges deriving from treaties or otherwise considered to the Greek and Bulgarian nationalities" in Macedonia. In regard to the referred editorial's statement that an independent Macedonia will provide a half solution which will make continuing trouble for the Allies, I beg to say that an independent Macedonia will be the surest basis for a lasting peace in the Balkans. Hitherto all the Balkan States have fought for the acquisition of Macedonia. The Bucharest treaty, which established the status quo ante bellum in the Balkans failed to bring a solution. King Carol of Rumania described it as "nothing more than a drumhead truce." The Carnegie Commission, which investigated the causes and the conduct of the Balkan wars, characterized it as the "illegitimate pretensions of victorious nationalities." Mr. Asquith, the English statesman, said: "The Bucharest treaty is founded on the ruins of violated contracts. It stands on the flimsy substructure of torn-up scraps of paper." It is evident from the above statements and the fact that Bulgaria joined the Central Powers to recover Macedonia that the best solution of the Balkan problem is to give an autonomy to Macedonia with the same form of government as that of Switzerland. The cantons, however, should be smaller in order to insure self-government for the various nationalities. An autonomous Macedonia will become a buffer State between Greece and Bulgaria and will provide a nucleus for a Balkan confederation – a confederation which will guarantee the future economic and intellectual development of the Balkans and which will be a barrier against anti-Balkan influences in the future. The independent Macedonia would have to be supervised for a time in order to be a success. The League of Nations should delegate a member from its own number with mandatory powers. Any of the European powers would be acceptable, but America would be the preferred member. The Macedonians have had enough experience with the European powers, whose main object has been to exploit their country. The United States has proved her disinterestedness in such matters in the Philippine Islands, Cuba, and Porto Rico. Besides, thousands of the Macedonians have resided in the United States for some time and know what it means to be under the control

of the American Government. An American Governor General who knows Eastern affairs intimately – a man like Mr. Henry Morgenthau, as some one has suggested – would go far to insure the success of the Macedonian State. An autonomy for Macedonia under American mandate will not be thrusting upon the people against their will something which they have not expressed desire for. They are in favor of some such a plan which will guarantee them the most elementary political rights. There has been formed recently in Switzerland a general council of the Macedonian societies, which has handed to the Premiers of the Entente Powers a memorandum in which the committee requested the following considerations – (1) Macedonia should be occupied by a combined army of American, English, French, and Italian troops; (2) All Macedonian refugees regardless of their faith or nationality should be allowed to return to their homes unmolested, and should be allowed to participate in the organization and management of their country's State affairs; (3) The local administration ;of Macedonia should be entrusted to the hands of the native inhabitants under the control of the army of occupation. The Macedonians in the United States have held two congresses. The first congress, which was held in Chicago, Ill., in 1913 unanimously adopted a resolution to demand religious and educational rights. The second congress was held last December, also in Chicago, Ill. The delegates adopted President Wilson's fourteen points by a unanimous rising vote. What the Macedonians of Switzerland and America – the only two countries where they can express their desires without any restraint – have said, is what they will continue to say and fight for, should their demands be not granted.
V.K. Sugareff. Cambridge, Mass., April 19, 1919.

1924 - *September 5th Callbran, Messa County: "Macedonia is for Republic Story of Conditions There Told by Emissary From the People". New York.* – A story of conditions in Macedonia, which he ascribes to Serb and Greek domination, has been brought to this country by J. Chkatroff, representative of the Union of the Macedonian Organizations of Bulgaria for the United States and Canada, who arrived here from Sofia recently. The Macedonians, he said, want complete independence and hope that ultimately there will be a Balkan republic, with all Balkan countries federated states. Mr. Chkatroff said he represented approximately 450,000 Macedonians in Bulgaria, who are members of 94 fraternal organizations, 34 societies of youths, a score of benevolent associations and others. He expects to bring his message of Macedonian hopes to the 60,000 natives of that country in the United States. 'In order to understand the causes of the unruly situation in the Balkans and especially in Macedonia, the country which has always been the apple of discord among the Balkan neighbors, one must not forget her struggle for liberty and political independence during the period of the Turkish domination, and the present-day policy of her new conquerors, Serbs and Greeks,' he said. Many years ago, the Macedonian people began a bloody revolutionary war, which has lasted already more than a quarter of a century, and this caused on several occasions the European chancelleries to move, and finally in 1912 the Balkan alliance was formed against the Turkish empire. Unfortunately, the first Balkan war, and the following fratricide among the Balkan allies culminating in the Treaty of Bucharest of 1913, instead of creating an independent Macedonia in accordance with the wishes of her people, and thus to establish a permanent peace in the Balkans, divided the country 39 between the three belligerents, Serbia, Greece, and Bulgaria. This actually made the Macedonian crisis worse. Errors Are Kept Up. The last European war which radically changed the map of Europe, and which gave us the great principles of self-determination of Woodrow Wilson, did not bring to the Macedonian question its deserved political solution. Macedonia, at that time, was waiting day and night to see those principles applied to her people, so that the latter may be able to freely determine their wishes as to the future of their country. But the Treaty of Peace of Neuilly (1919) seconded the grave errors committed by the Treaty of Bucharest. "It is true that the great victorious powers imposed upon the governments of Serbia and Greece a treaty for the protection of minorities, which was supposed to guarantee the minimum of political, civil and national rights of the Macedonians. This treaty has now become as valueless as a scrap of paper. The Serbian and Greek governments instead of creating a normal regime in Macedonia as soon as they reoccupied the country after the great war closed by force more than 1,400 Bulgaro-Macedonian schools with 80,000 pupils and more than 4,000 teachers, which were devotedly supported and financed by the local population; seized the Macedonian churches. Libraries and cultural institutions; burned all Bulgarian books and killed or banished from the country all of the Macedonian intelligentsia. Nor was the fate of our other compatriots, Turks, and Rumanians, in Macedonia a better one. The heavy fetters of the Serbian and Greek tyranny are to be found today on the doors of the closed Rumanian and Turkish schools and public libraries in Macedonia. In addition to this policy of the Serbian and Greek governments, which is directed against the moral and intellectual institutions of the Macedonian people, following the practice of former Turkish governments, they began to use new means and methods in order to artificially change the ethnographic character of the country; they resorted to a policy of colonization. Today Serbian and Greek authorities deport the native Macedonian population, plunder their property, and distribute same among colonists brought from Banat and Asia Minor. To have an idea of the terrible picture one must visit the thousands of recently arrived refugees, flying from Macedonia into Bulgaria, a country economically poor, and see their tortured bodies burned with hot irons or boiling oil. There are two further reasons which aggravate the situation in Macedonia. First, there is a Serbian and Greek administration, whose 40 officers are alien to the people; notorious corruption and sheer force are the only rules in the country, and it seems that the whip is their constitution. One could find out proofs of this by reading Serbian and Greek newspapers. Secondly, the newly created political frontiers tore away the economic bonds between Macedonian cities and districts. Serbian Macedonia has no sea outlet and is gradually dying. Greek Macedonia has no "hinterland," while the remaining part of Macedonia – under Bulgarian authority – has neither sea nor any convenient land communications with the interior of that country, and for this reason, is in a worse condition. The principle economical and political center in Macedonia is Saloniki, which has all the advantages of prosperity, yet at present the city gradually, but certainly, is dying. Her people do not see any more the steaming boats, the commerce is dead, and the merchants are leaving the town. Pathras and Pereas are rising on her ruins. Bitola, Prilep, Ochrid and many other towns are sharing the same fate. Under such heavy conditions could the Macedonian people remain quiet? With their country torn into pieces could they forget the thousands of lives sacrificed for the liberty and independence of Macedonia, ever since the days of the Turkish regime? Who could deny the right of the Macedonian to struggle for existence? Who could forbid the Macedonians the fruit of their labors so that the latter may not be plundered by Serbian and Greek authorities and the Macedonian girls and brides may not be insulted by the same? And the Macedonian did exactly as an American, Frenchman or an Englishman would have done. The whole people were frightened by the terror of the new tyranny and rose up to protest. Banished from their own country, the Macedonians found refuge in Bulgaria, America, Turkey and Rumania, where they formed strong organizations whose aim is by legal means to obtain liberty for their country. The

Macedonian emigrants in all lands, who number more than half a million souls, proclaimed their faith in the traditions of past generations and now appeal continuously to the human conscience of the civilized people in the world for the creation of Macedonia into a free country. Old Revolutionary System. Meanwhile in Macedonia proper, after denying the people all rights of carrying a legal political struggle or forming a national political group in the parliament of Belgrade and Athens, they resorted to the only possible action by creating anew the old secret revolutionary organization with its own postal service, courts, militia and efficiently armed military forces, with its own educational and economic policy – in other words, representing a true state organization, mysterious, yet powerful and democratic in spirit, whose ideals are the creation of an independent Macedonia with equal rights for all of her different nationalities, with Saloniki as her capital. The Macedonians are neither brigands nor breakers of the laws governing public order and safety, when they are ready to sacrifice their lives for the triumph of their ideals, when they gladly go to die in order to defend their wives and children, when they calmly meet death in order to save Macedonia. And in their struggle for right and freedom the Macedonians hope that they may receive the support of all civilized nations and all liberty-loving people." (*The Plateau Voice, Callbran, Messa County, Friday, September 5th, 1924, page 3*)

1924 – September 16th Sofia, Bulgaria New York Times: "MACEDONIAN LEADERS MURDERED ALEXANDROFF DEAD". *(From our correspondent). SOFIA, September 15.* – Todor Alexanderoff, the Macedonian leader, was assassinated on August 31 by Macedonian opponents who had lately come under Bolshevist influence. News has been received at the Bulgarian Legation that Aleko Pash and Colonel Athanasoff, two prominent members of the Macedonian Revolutionary

Organization, have been murdered at Gorna Jumaya, in South-Western Bulgaria. At the same time two leaders of the Macedonian Federalists have been killed in Sofia. Todor Alexandroff who was born in 1882, was one of the most picturesque leaders in the Balkans. He began life as a school master but soon forsook this profession for the more war like one of komitaji (political brigand). He took part in the continuous struggle which the Macedonians waged against the Turks, but in 1913 his health gave away and he went to France. During the European War he belonged to the Macedonian Division which operated against the allies on the Struma front and worked for the Germans as a spy. After the war he sank into comparative obscurity, but when the Treaty of Neuilly was signed, in November 1919, dividing the greater part of Macedonia between Yugoslavia and Greece, Alexandroff resumed his crusade for an autonomous Macedonia. Together with General Protogeroff and Peter Chauleff, Alexandroff directed the policy of the Revolutionary Organization, and roamed the countryside to keep the revolutionary spirit alive. Possessed of a most magnetic presence, Alexandroff, as the writer knew him, was the type of fanatical patriot who would stop at nothing to achieve his goal – the creation of an autonomous Macedonia. He had undoubtedly been responsible for many assassinations, and it is therefore not to be wondered at that he himself came to a violent end. It is too early to say what the effect of his death would be, but General Protogeroff is likely to take his place as revolutionary leader. An account of an interview between Todor Alexandroff and a correspondent, which took place a month ago in the mountains of Macedonia, will be found on p. 9."
(*The New York Times, September 16, 1924*)

1924 – September 16th New York Times: "MACEDONIAN AIMS MURDERED LEADER'S DECLARATION". (From a Correspondent.) In August I had a nocturnal interview with Alexandroff in the mountains of Macedonia in a spot some distance from the Bulgarian frontier, where we were surrounded by Komitajis armed to the teeth. I was anxious to find out to what extent the Macedonian Revolutionary was in alliance with the Bolshevists, who had announced in their organ, La Federation Balkanique, which is published in Vienna, that the Macedonian chiefs had signed a manifesto strongly supporting the policy of the Soviet for the overthrow of all existing Balkan Governments. It was reported that two at least of the Macedonian Triumvirate, Alexanderoff and Protogueroff had denounced this manifesto referred to in the Times of August 5 and 6, as a forgery, and the only means of obtaining definite information on this point was to get it from Alexandroff himself. In reply to my question, the Macedonian leader said: - I declare that I did not sign either the manifesto published in La Federation Balkanique and attributed by that review to the Central Committee of the Macedonian Organization, nor have I signed any other similar documents. If my signature is at the bottom, of this manifesto, it is false; Protogeroff also affirms that he has not signed this manifesto. We have no desire to struggle against European capitalism, which does not concern us. The Organization has only one aim: the liberation of Macedonia. And as long as I am alive, and as long as I am at the head of the Organization, I shall not allow the Organization to fall away from this its fundamental and only aim and to become an instrument for aims which are strange to it. The Organization has nothing in common with Communism and Bolshevism. I do not deny the fact that the Bolshevists have tried several times to win over the Organization and in every occasion it is they who have taken the initiative in negotiating. It was after an order received from Moscow that the Bulgarian Communist Press ceased to attack us in 1922, although we did not ask anyone to spare us the attacks of the Communist papers. In 1923 the Soviet agents again proposed to me to begin negotiations. I then put the following conditions as an essential preliminary to the negotiations; The dissolution of Pandurski's Communist band, the suppression of the Macedonian Communist paper Osvobojdenje, and the dissolution of the Communist organization of the Macedonian émigrés. My ultimatum was accepted and fully executed in August 1923, but in September of the same year there was the rising of the Agrarians and Communists in Bulgaria and I had declared to the Communists that I consider all risings and coup d'etat complicated the already difficult position in Bulgaria and were injurious and inadmissible. In the name of the Organization, I informed the Communists that the independence of Bulgaria was extremely dear to me and as a Communist coup d'etat would threaten this independence, the Organization would be obliged to consider every attempt to overthrow the existing Government and to substitute for it a Government of Communists and Agrarians as a blow to the independence of Bulgaria, and that consequently it will begin a direct and pitiless struggle with the authors of such attempts and will deal with them as it deals with all its enemies. It will be understood that after such a declaration negotiations could not be continued. 'LEFT' ELEMENTS. But I do not deny that in our Organization there are 'Left' elements who invariably say that during five years we have not been able to obtain anything from the League of Nations, Paris, or London, and that consequently we must try and come into an agreement with Moscow. Under the influence of the 'Left', but, again, on the initiatives of the Soviet representatives in Vienna, negotiations were began in 1924. The representative of the Soviet of Moscow put as a condition for an agreement with us the consent of the Organization to the 'Sovietizing' of Bulgaria and Macedonia. We replied that this condition was unacceptable to us and negotiations ceased.

Since then, they have not again been resumed. In London I did not see Rakovski, and I did not sign any agreement with him. Information concerning this agreement probably comes from the same origin as the manifesto. I repeat that, as long as I remain at the head of the Organization, the latter will fight by all means against Bolshevism, which, in my opinion, is greatly injurious to the national Macedonian movement. And again, a few days ago, I informed the Bulgarian Communists, in the name of the Organization, that the Organization will not permit a Communist coup d'etat in Bulgaria. But I must say that the situation in Macedonia becomes intolerable. From the memorandum which the Organization will present to the League of Nations in September, Europe will be able to convince itself that the Serbian and Greek regimes are worse than the Turkish. For the Serbian and Greek regimes by their cruelty, illegality, and violence surpass anything that can be imagined. As long as these continue and as long as Macedonia is governed by barbarous methods, the Organization will not desist from its armed struggle; on the contrary, its struggle will be increased. But we shall willingly put aside our arms and begin a political and cultural existence as soon as the necessary conditions for free political and cultural development are guaranteed to the Macedonian population. CONDITIONS DEMANDED. Our requests are very modest. We do not want the dissolution of Yugoslavia; we desire that Yugoslavia becomes a Federal, free, and strong State. And in the name of the Organization, I formally declare that the Organization will cease its armed struggle if the following conditions are fulfilled:

(*The New York Times, September 16, 1924*)

-

1. The dissolution of subsidized Serbian official bands of Stoyan Micheff, Zikleff and other traitors throughout Macedonia and the prosecution of the members of these bands for the crimes which they have committed (rape, assassinations and brigandage).

2. The application of the clauses included in the Peace Treaty for the defense of the rights of National Minorities under the control of the League of Nations and under the guarantee of the Great Powers.

3. An amnesty of all arrested Macedonians and the permission to return to Macedonia the refugees and émigrés also under the control of the League of Nations and the guarantee of the Great Powers.

4. The liberty of elections in the Skupshtina and the granting of the Macedonians to the right to form legal political parties. These are our fundamental requests, and if our demands are executed in a strict, loyal, and honest manner, we engage ourselves to put aside our arms and to cease our armed struggle. We also insist in the same way as other people included in Yugoslavia in the reconstruction of Yugoslavia into a federal state in which Macedonia would enter as a member of the Federation on equal rights with other members of the Yugoslav Federation. Taking into consideration the inevitable decomposition in the near future of Greece we ask the incorporation of the Autonomous Macedonia of the Macedonian territory which is now under the Greek dominion. When all the above conditions are sincerely and honestly executed the part of Macedonia which is in the hands of Bulgaria must also be incorporated into the Autonomous Macedonia. I am convinced that it is only in this way and acting as I have indicated that it will be possible to avoid Bolshevism in

the Balkan Peninsula, that peace will be insured in the Balkans, and that a strong and durable Yugoslavia will be created. The duty of the Western European Democracies, in which we still have faith, is to save Macedonia from death and the Macedonian population from destruction, or, which is the same thing, from Bolshevism."
(*The New York Times, September 16, 1924*)

1925 - *April 25th Chillicoth Missouri:* "EUROPE LEARNS NOTHING FROM THE WORLD WAR" "To the Southeast, in the Balkans, the familiar signs of unrest are not lacking. Belgrade has resorted to dictatorship. Jugoslavia and Bulgaria watch one other across their frontiers, wondering which will leave the first brick. The Macedonians continue their policy of provoking first the Serbs and then the Bulgarians in the hope that someday, while the two are quarreling, Macedonia will run off with the coveted bone of independence." (*The Daily Constitution, Chillicothe, Missouri, Wednesday, April 25th, 1925*)

1934 – *June 26th Reno, Nevada:* "THE CULT OF ALEXANDER" It is not only Mussolini who is harking back to the ancient Romans for a means of inspiring modern Italy, or Hitler who turns to the old-time Teutons to give a model for the modern German. Greece begins to realize that it has heroes of its own and now General George Condylis, minister of War at Athens places his candidate for adulation before the descendents of the old Hellenes. It is no less a person than Alexander the Great. Condylis proposes to erect the ideal of Alexander into a real cult. A statue is to be raised to him at once in Athens, lectures have been organized at the university and schools, and the Alexandrian tactics and conquests are being studied as a means of giving the modern Greek some conception of what it meant to be one of his nations 2200 years ago. Which is all very well, but the truth is that the ancient Greeks scarcely admitted

Alexander to be one of their blood. He was a Macedonian. The Athenians fought against allowing his father to enter their territory and the orations against Philip delivered by Demosthenes are regarded today as the most magnificent specimens of oratory. They have given a name to denunciatory speeches – Philippics. Alexander, it is true, overcame all this but he had to conquer the real Greeks to do it. His phalanx was a Macedonian phalanx and not a Greek one. His lieutenants and successors were Macedonians and not Greeks, although they spoke Greek and worshipped Greek gods. And as for Macedonia, it is even yet an uncertain possession either of Greece or Bulgaria. It still tries to be independent."
(*Reno Evening Gazette, Reno Nevada, Thursday, June 26th, 1934, page 5*)

1935 – May 27th Massillon, Ohio: "Macedonians to have convention". The Macedonian People's league will hold its fifth annual convention at the German-American hall. 834 Grant St., Akron. Thursday, Friday, Saturday and Sunday. Approximately 100 delegates representing 36 groups in the United States and Canada with a membership of 1,200 will attend. Activities of the League will be discussed and a concrete plan for future campaigns in support of the struggle of the Macedonian people for a free Macedonia will be worked out. Thursday, the central committee will give out its annual report. That evening at 8 o'clock a banquet in honor of delegates and guests will be held. One of the features of the convention will be a mass demonstration from Perkins square to Pleasant Park against the national and social oppression of the Macedonian people by the governments of Yugoslavia, Greece and Bulgaria, Sunday at 2 p.m. Besides the delegates and guests, many Akron workers and immigrants from the Balkan organizations will take part in the demonstration. Prominent speakers will have addresses." (*The Evening Independent, Massillon, Ohio, Monday, May 27, 1935*).

1939 – *April 1ˢᵗ Newark, Ohio:* "*GREEK CHURCH PLANS SERVICES*" Service next week in the Roumanian church, of the Greek Orthodox faith, was announced today. Service will be held Thursday, Friday, and Saturday at 9 a.m. and Sunday at 8 a.m. in the church at Wirlwood and Poplar avenues. In addition to morning session, a service will be held on Thursday at 6 p.m. Rev. D. Justremicean of Detroit will conduct the services. It was announced that all Rumanians, Macedonians, Greeks, Bulgarians and Serbians are invited to attend."
(*The Advocate, Newark, Ohio, April 1st, 1939, page 3*)

1940 – *September 3ʳᵈ New York:* "Macedonian League Urges its Members to back U.S. Defense" Buffalo, Sept. 3. – Americans of Macedonian descent are urged in a resolution of the Macedonian People's League of the United States. The resolution, adopted at the closing session of the League's annual convention yesterday, also favors support for the national defense program 'as long as it does not encourage fighting abroad'. Snearie Voyeanoss, Pontiac, Mich., was re-elected national chairman, and Garry, Ind., was chosen for the 1940 meeting. Other officers are George Pirinsky, Detroit, Mich., national secretary; Dr. George Popoff, Buffalo, Michael Jovaehess, Detroit, Mich., William Popoff, Garry, Ind., Thomas Tavgos, Massillon, O., and William Goushiess, Mediscon, Dl., directors."
(*Syracuse Herald Journal, Tuesday, September 3rd, 1940*)

1940 – *November 8ᵗʰ Sofia, Bulgaria:* "Defenders Hold Balance, Metaxas Tells People" Sofia, Bulgaria, Nov 8 (BUP). – Primier Metaxas of Greece broadcast over the radio in Athen's tonight that after ten days of Italo-Greek warfare the balance was in Greece's favour. The Greek radio said that British aid is flowing to Greece 'regularly and according to plan.' Metaxas, addressing his remarks to the town of Volos after it had been bombed from the air, asserted that 'Italian methods will stir our people to fight even with greater recklessness and courage until the last battle is won.' He declared Italy had resorted to 'mean, base methods' by attacking civilian populations of open towns. Metaxas said proof that the balance lay with Greece could be seen in the number of prisoners taken and the penetration of Albania. The Athens radio 'regretted' that the Italians found Greek roads very bad and the weather inferior, asserting, however, that the Greeks have found them both good enough to advance as far as the heights above Koritza. The broadcast denied vigorously Italian allegations that Macedonians had revolted against Greek rule, and rumours that prince Paul had been mistreated for supposed pro-German sympathies and had fled to Canada." (*Globe and Mail, November 8th, 1940*)

1945 – *June 27th Melbourne, Australia: "BANDS OF GREEKS TERRORIZE MACEDONIANS"* Yugoslav Charges Allegations in Yugoslav newspapers that bands of Greek left-wing guerrillas, under the command of General Zervas are making terror attacks against Macedonians have given rise to fears that international complications maybe in the making, says Associated Press Belgrade correspondent, - AAP." (*The Argus, Melbourne, Australia, Wednesday, June 27, 1945, page 1*)

1945 - *August 24th Iowa: "Macedonia Asks for Autonomy One of Greatest Trouble Spots" SALONIKA, Greece:* - Local patriots are reviving the old cry for autonomy for Macedonia, an ill-defined area in the heart of the troubled Balkans. Macedonia, which has not enjoyed a national sovereignty since the time of Alexander the Great, today is one of the greatest potential trouble spots in Europe. The country is divided into three parts. It comprises a large part of Northern Greece and Southern Yugoslavia and a small section of Bulgaria. Gathered here are representatives of all the races and most of the hatreds and tensions which have kept the Balkan Peninsula upset for 50 years.

Greek-Yugoslav relations are strained along the common frontier which cuts through the wild mountains of Macedonia as a result of the depredation of political and bandit bands. Greeks say there is evidence of recruiting by irregular Macedonian forces. The autonomy campaign is in the open in Yugoslavia and Bulgaria and is underground in Greece. Yugoslav Macedonia, formerly known as South Serbia, has been given a type of autonomy under Marshal Tito's framework of federated Yugoslavia. This is a step in the direction the autonomists want, and agitation for union of all parts under a single government follows almost automatically.

Will be approved by Greece. In the early days of liberation, the Yugoslav Macedonians attempted to name a foreign minister of their own. There was quick reaction from Belgrade, and Skopje, their capital was given a new set of government officials with strict instructions that foreign policy was the province of the central government. Greeks look on any effort towards an autonomous Macedonia as a threat to take from them the rich farmlands of the north upon which the whole national economy depends. Far from listening to the demands, Greece will probably seek at the peace conferences to extend her frontier northward. Bulgaria gave lip service to the autonomy principle during the war years when her troops occupied much of Greek and Yugoslav Macedonia. But the real intention of the occupation troops, it became evident, was to Bulgarize the whole area. Many autonomists then joined the partisan resistance forces." (*Council Bluffs Iowa, Nonpareil, Friday, August 24th, 1945, page 9*)

1947 - April 26*th* Athens, Greece in the New York Times: *"Macedonians Executed"* ATHENS, April 25 (Reuters) – Twenty guerrillas were shot by a firing squad at Kozani, Western

Macedonia, today after being sentenced for alleged membership in a 'Slav Macedonian armed band'. The organization was accused of autonomist activities in Macedonia. Seven communists were sentenced to death by a court-martial at Mytiline for activities endangering the state. The Greek General Staff has filed an espionage charge against the management of the Athens newspaper Rizospastis, organ of the Greek communist party, which published an alleged top secret army report on the strength and organization of the guerrilla forces in Greece." (*The New York Times, April 26, 1947*)

1947 – June 8th Athens, Greece in the New York Times: "Greece Executes 8 Macedonians". ATHENS. June 7 (Reuthers) – Eight Macedonian civilians sentenced to death by a court-martial on charges of plotting to separate Macedonia from Greece were shot at Salonika today. They were said to have been members of a 'terroristic' Slav organization."
(*The New York Times, June 8, 1947*).

"The Greeks had not taken much interest in their past until Europeans became enthusiastic discoverers and diggers of their ruins. And why should they have cared? The Greeks were not Greek but the illiterate descendants of Slavs and Albanian fishermen, who spoke a debased Greek dialect and had little interest in the broken columns and temples except as places to graze their sheep. The true philhellenes were the English – of whom Byron was the epitome – and the French, who were passionate to link themselves with the Greek ideal. This rampant and irrational phili-Hellenism, which amounted almost to a religion, was also a reaction to the confident dominance of the Ottoman Turks, who were widely regarded as savages and heathens. The Turks had brought their whole culture, their language, their Muslim religion and their distinctive cuisine not only here but throughout the Middle East and into Europe as far as Budapest. The contradiction persists even today: Greek food is actually Turkish food, and many words we think as distinctively Greek, are in reality Turkish – kebab, doner, kofta, meze, teramasalata, dolma, yogurt, moussaka, and so forth; all Turkish." *("The Pillars of Hercules", by Paul Theroux, page 316)*

'Greece is the most artificial of all artificial nations that resulted from the dissolution of the Ottoman Empire.' Yerasimos Kaklamanis
(*Analysis of Neohellenic Bourgeois Ideology, page 13*).

"Argolida has been continuously settled since ancient times. Since the Mycenaean era, it has been under the continual occupation of successive empires and states, from the city-states of ancient Greece through Rome and Byzantium, the Venetians, Ottomans and finally the modern Greek state. Successive waves of conquerors and immigrants have all left their mark. Today the area is widely considered to be the heartland of modern Greece. The revolution that lead to the founding of the modern Greek state in 1821 was centered in the Peloponessos, and Nauplio became its first capital. Since then, the construction of Greek national identity has tended to efface processes of social differentiation. The institutions and ideology of the Greek nation-state have sought to project an unproblematic narrative of Greek history stretching back to ancient times (Herzfeld 1982).

Despite these efforts, however, it is difficult to document a continuous lineage of 'Greek' identity. Instead, what we find is a history of confrontation, contradiction and assimilation among contentious social groups and ethnic identities. The notion of a 'Greek' identity in the modern sense is itself in large part a creation of the movement towards statehood. It was not until the nineteenth century that the term came to describe a homogenous ethnic group in the modern sense. Instead, the peoples of the Peloponnesus, including Argolida, made up an intricate mosaic of ethnicities and languages. In Argolida dialects of Albanian, Greek, Turkish and other local languages were spoken (*Andromedas 1976*).

From the Byzantine Empire and onwards, religion was an important marker of social identity. The Byzantines were Greek speakers, but they associated the Greek language with Christianity rather than ancient Greece, and in fact ethnically defined themselves as 'Romans', a term carried over to the Ottoman Empire as 'Rum' meaning Orthodox Christians." *("Blood and Oranges Immigrant Labour and European Markets in Rural Greece", by Christopher M. Lawrence, page 12)*

"Angolida, like the coastal areas of the Peloponnesus in general, has a long history of invasions and immigration due to the economic significance of the area and its location along the eastern Mediterranean trade routes. The three villages of Agia Triada, Manesi and Gerbisi all trace their history back to the decline of the Byzantine Empire. The original name of Agia Triada was Merbeka, probably derived from the surname of the Catholic bishop of Corinth during the Frankish crusader state, Wilhelm von Moerbeke, who established the Deocesan seat there in 1277 (*Salapatas 2000*).

It is mentioned in a census of 1700 as containing thirty families and 157 residents.
In 1817 it is listed as having 160 residents. In 1834, Merbeka was incorporated as a town (dimos) with a population of 320 (*Skiadas 1993*).

Gerbesi and Manesi both seem to have been founded in the sixteenth century when the area was under Venetian control. Both names apparently refer to immigrant Albanian soldiers working for the Venetians that also appear as names of villages in what is today as southern Albania.
(*Mauros 1980*).

Albanian speakers moved into Argolida in several waves in the next centuries, creating differences that are perceived today. Residents of Garbesi are thought to share lineage with the people of Limnes, a village some 20 kilometres away, while the villages of Prosomni and Arachneo are thought to represent a later immigration. Residents of Garbesi often cite this history in explaining inter village differences and conflicts. In the early 1950's the names of Merbeka and Garbesi were changed to the more 'Greek sounding' Agia Triada (meaning Holy Trinity) and Midea (from the Mycenaean site), the culmination of a long process of cultural homogenization initiated by the emergence of the modern Greek state in 1821. Manesi, for unexplainable reasons, was allowed to keep its Arvanitiko name." *("Blood and Oranges Immigrant Labour and European Markets in Rural Greece", by Christopher M. Lawrence, page 13)*

If we must believe we have to engage in any old rubbish about who "invented" the Macedonians with any of our appalling opponents, especially the Greeks, let me run some thoughts past you I have had of late and also what I think about the Tito thesis: If Tito could have created a "Macedonian ethnic group" with a Macedonian language and history, he was or is probably as good as any saint or miracle worker in the best religions of the world.

So, let me repeat what I once proposed to our Greek friends on a moronic blog 52 site when I was still naïve and believed that the Internet could be a force for deliberative democracy: the Greeks should build and have consecrated by the Patriarch in Istanbul (no longer Constantinople, alas, for the day in 1453) a holy cathedral. Now this cathedral should be built in Greek-occupied Macedonia (Let us never forget since 1913) in honour of Saint Josip Broz Tito who performed the miracle of creating an ethnic group called "Macedonian".

The reason for the "Greeks" (who created *them*, by the way?) consecrating such a cathedral "our Dedo" in historical Macedonian territory is that modern Greeks can pray to Saint J B Tito with their usual fervour for a "Macedonian" ethnic group to be delivered to them which speaks Greek. (Incidentally, the fact that Tito was a communist and an atheist who used the excuse for his policies "Narodot" rather than "Boga" is just a point of historical detail - a saint must make the most of his opportunities.)

If anyone really wants to know who "created" the Macedonians let them consider the following line of argument: Aristotle the philosopher (384-322 B.C) born in Stageira in the ancient kingdom of Macedonia had his mental or psychic structure formed by a Macedonian upbringing of the time. He became learned in every area of human knowledge in the Attic language (not called "Greek" at the time) in the city state of Athens. He has been the most extraordinary and most influential thinker in European civilization and beyond. Aristotle's thought and writings were rescued by brilliant Arab philosophers like Averroes, Avicenna etc. and his influence came into the medieval world via the Arabic language, then Latin, Spanish Castilian, etc., so he was a universal genius that could speak to humanity in all languages.

His basic view was intellectualist: that through the use of reason human beings could find happiness. And yes, he was a

Macedonian, not an Athenian, and I would choose him as my model rather than Alexander the Great and not just because I happen to have been born about 150 kilometres from Stageira in the middle of the 20th century. (Incidentally, Alexander the Great died at the age of 32 of alcoholic poisoning because the Macedonians and the "Greeks" were not convinced that he should be worshipped as a god - an idea about kingship that he keenly adopted from the more profound and complex cultures he had conquered in the East). I think it is important to remind ourselves that the real world beyond the Balkan nationalistic propaganda fantasyland does not care about who the real descendants are from the "cradle of culture".

So shoulder to the wheel let us again speak of the key priorities: human and national rights for the Macedonians in 2009. The justice and freedom that they are entitled to at present and should be striving for 53 are not even remotely connected to issues concerning antiquity or even Sveti Dedo Tito (Holy grandfather Tito). Although, I do commend the unmasking of the claptrap and hocus pocus of the nationalists - it is the positive stuff that should be fore grounded rather than the lies that every nation feels obliged to tell to bolster itself up as a legitimate entity. (*Aleksandar Donski 2009*).

So, to all those out there parroting the nonsense that "Macedonians are an invention of Tito" and didn't exist prior to 1945; The name Macedonia has been irrefutably pointed out throughout this book by orators, by historians, by major news publications and authors alike contemporary and ancient over the course of thousands of years – whereas Tito died in 1983.

Simon Tasievski

REGARDING ENTRY TO NATO, THE EU AND THE UN

The fact is that every single nation agreed to the name Republic of Macedonia, and that it was **only** Greece that had vetoed it for reasons we have already outlined in detail. Without a unanimous decision we are now at this junction. The name changed to North Macedonia **without** a vote and against the wishes of its population who were strongly against it. The leaders are corrupt, plain and simple.

Now it's Bulgaria's turn playing tag-team with Greece to prevent Macedonia from entering with absolutely absurd and ridiculous demands that even the simplest of idiots would still **never** agree to. There is a reason for this – keep Macedonia out and delegitimize them at all costs!

The EU UN and NATO are all in bed with one other, of which none of the representatives are elected or chosen by people so who are they to possibly govern or dictate terms to anyone about anything?

The exact reason why the Euro is dying so soon after its conception, economy's failing with countries such as Portugal, Italy, Ireland, Spain, and at the very top of the list is Greece.

Macedonia is an indisputable, integral, and the only country that has existed from Europe's inception since prehistory, so to say that "Macedonia isn't in Europe" because of politics regarding the UN, the EU and NATO are complete nonsense.

Macedonia: A History

CONCLUSION

We know who we are, and we know where we come from. The very reason Bulgaria and Greece want to keep what they stole/annexed from us, and yes, it was stolen, is that there are thousands of maps from numerous countries all over the world, all showing Macedonia's correct borders which differ vastly from prior to 1912 to that of today.

The Treaty of Bucharest confirms such maps and the subsequent divisions of land, along with the countless newspaper publications and references to "Macedonia" since prehistory.

Over the last 100 years or so, both Greece and Bulgaria had spent hundreds of millions, possibly even into the billions of dollars in infrastructure into the stolen Macedonian land, as technology had evolved and changed significantly since 1913 to what we have available to us today – note that we are talking about our country being annexed in the days of horse and cart, no cars, no indoor plumbing, no electricity etc. and then *only* since 1995 with the collapse of the former Yugoslavia realizing "oh crap, we may possibly now have to return this land soon..."

So, their theory runs along the thought process that if the name changes as they would very much like it to, then the narrative for them also changes to "well that new country/name didn't exist when we 'attained' it back in 1913, so now there's no one to return it to so therefore it will remain ours".

This is the entire reasoning behind the strong push for name change and so-called "name dispute".
There is no name dispute. We are Macedonians.
Modern Greece likes to believe it somehow owns the entire world and can dictate terms.

Cyprus and a *lot* of the islands such as Rhodes, Lesbos, Samos or Kos for example off the coast of Turkey, are *much* closer to Turkey than they are to Greece which is hundreds and hundreds of kilometers away, whereas some islands can be seen or even swam to from mainland Turkey. How are they possibly "Greek islands" when they are nowhere even near mainland Greece?

Then come the claims of "Magna Grecia!" (Greater Greece). So, we're to understand that the Italians are now somehow Greek too then right (according to them), because in ancient times of trade they could speak Koine and people traveled there? Same as Egypt, same as Africa etc.
Hellenism and the Hellenistic era are exactly that – just an era, a large nondescript region and in no logical way a country called Greece that had borders.

Lebanon, which in ancient times was called Phoenicia, is also considered as being 'Hellenic'. Are they Greek now too? The pillars of Hercules between Spain and Morocco, (Hercules being the Latin form of the name which it is called), over 4,000kms away are they also Greeks now too?

The Hellespont/Dardanelles between European and Asian Turkey (Asia Minor) where the Koine language was spoken much like the entirety of Europe are all supposedly Greek too according to them right?

Do they not see the absolute absurdity of such nonsense claims?

Simon Tasievski

THERE CANNOT BE AN ANCIENT VERSION OF A MODERN COUNTRY, IT'S AS SIMPLE AS THAT

No one says ancient Italy when referring to Rome, Venetians, or Florentines.
No one says ancient Lebanon when referring to Phoenicia.
No one says ancient Iran when referring to Persia.
No one says ancient France when referring to Gaul.
No one says ancient Serbia when referring to Illyria.
No one says ancient Bulgaria when referring to Thrace.
No one says ancient Iraq when referring to Babylon/Sumeria/Mesopotamia etc.
No one says ancient Spain when referring to Iberia.
No one says ancient Turkey when referring to the Hittites.
No one says ancient Russia when referring to the Scythians.
No one says ancient Tunisia when referring to Carthage.
No one says ancient Germany when referring to the Bavarians.
No one says ancient Czech Republic when referring to Bohemia.

There is no such place as ancient Greece, it only became 'Greece' as a country in 1830 so people really need to stop repeating and saying this nonsense.

3,000 years ago, the name, the language, and the identity of the people called themselves Macedonians.

1,000 years ago, the name, the language, and the identity of the people called themselves Macedonians.

100 years ago, the name, the language, and the identity of the people called themselves Macedonians.

To this day, there are people in the occupied territories within both Greece and Bulgaria slowly coming out from under the shadow of the last centuries world wars and dictatorships, who have kept their name, kept their language, and kept their identity as Macedonian.

To this very day in 2025, within both Pirin Macedonia and Aegean Macedonia (Bulgaria and Greece), we have absolutely no problem at all speaking the Macedonian language and being completely understood by the local population. Macedonian dances and festivals have even slowly started being performed by people here because of technology, the internet, live social media videos and having less fear from the government as they know that the world is now constantly watching so there's that added layer of protection for them.

The people know who they are, they know where they are from, and they know their language. They are Macedonians.

Greece and Bulgaria have been trying to wipe out the Macedonian name and identity ever since they annexed lands that did not belong to them since 1913, and have done everything they possibly can to eradicate, delete, and wipe any possible trace of Macedonia away for good.

But this hasn't happened, nor will it **ever** happen.

There are only 3 countries in all of recorded history in the world today which have never been known as anything else ever since prehistory.

Every other country on Earth has either changed its name, been previously known as something different, been overruled, or simply wiped out completely at some point in time in the past.

These three countries are Egypt, China, and Macedonia.

Egypt has always been Egypt.
China has always been China, and
Macedonia has always been Macedonia.

Only Macedonia - Never North
Macedonia for the Macedonians

Simon Tasievski

Macedonia: A History

Simon Tasievski

ACKNOWLEDGEMENTS

As well as the myriads of authors that have already been mentioned and quoted within this book, there are a few here that deserve special mention.

These are the authors that I have taken great inspiration from and have paraphrased, who contributed a great volume of the content within that I simply could not have completed this book without the help of. I will list a number of suggested reading from these authors that provide further in-depth information into each specific topic, which can be found online in e-book version.

These notable authors are as follows:

Most notably: Risto Stefov, Ernst Badian, Eugene N. Borza, Tome Bosevski & Aristotel Tentov, Aleksandar Donski, Krste Misirkov, Jason Miko, Stoian Kochov, Dr. Prof. Kosta Peev, Odyssey Belstone Belchevsky, Risto Nikovski, Danny Ben-Moshe Associate Professor Deakin University, Dr Joanne Pyke, Victoria University, Mr Ordan Andreevski - United Macedonian Diaspora, Jim Hlavac, Prof. Dr. Christian Voß, Humboldt-Universität zu Berlin Institut für Slawistik, George V Durtanosky, Norm Mitsopoulos, Basil Chulev, Spiro Mavrovski, Giorgio Nurigiani, Prof. Paul Cutter, Aneta Shukarova, Ph.D., Mitko B. Panov, Ph.D., Dragi Georgiev, Ph.D., Krste Bitovski, Ph.D.,

Academician Ivan Katardziev, Vanche Stojchev, Ph.D., Novica Veljanovski, Ph.D., Todor Chepreganov, Ph.D., A. Arnaiz-Villena, K. Dimitroski , J. Moscoso, E. Go´mez-Casado, C. Silvera-Redondo, P. Varela, M. Blagoevska, V. Zdravkovska, J. Martı´nez-Laso, Martin Trenevski, Horace G Lunt, Todor Hristov Simovski, Atanas Tane Naumovski, Elizabeth Stewart (nee Kolupacev), Stoian Georgiev Tomovichin, ACAD. Antonije Skokljev Donco, Slave Nikoloski-Katin, Lena Jankovski, Alex Bakratcheff, Dr. Mihailo Minoski, Pascal Kamburovski, Victor Sinadinoski, Kosta Mundushev, Viktor Lilchikj Adams, Igor Shirtovski, Vladimir Atanasov, Viktor Simonovski, Filip Adzievski, Dimitar Mirchev, Turkkaya Ataov, Petre Nakovski, Zhidas Daskalovski, Marija Risteska, Biljana Vankovska, Aleksandar Mitreski, Nedzad Mehmedovic, Didem Ekinci, Dragan Tevdovski, Christopher K. Lamont, Evdokia Foteva – Vera, Branko Sotirovski

Simon Tasievski

RECOMMENDED & SUGGESTED READING — ALL AVAILABLE IN E-BOOK AND MOSTLY FOR FREE BY THESE AUTHORS

On Macedonian Matters - Krste Misirkov 1903

DENYING ETHNIC IDENTITY - The Macedonians of Greece

2018 Annual Report on the Human Rights Situation of the Macedonian Minority in Bulgaria

A Century Of Silence 1913-2013

The Proto Slavic Macedonian Meaning Of The Names From The Trojan Wars Homeric Age

America's Role In Macedonia's Troubled Journey To International Recognition

Analysis of historical events in Greek occupied Macedonia 1 & 2

Ancient Macedonians were not Greeks

ARC Macedonian-diaspora in Australia report

Australian Macedonians and their language(s)

Bronze Age Europe Animal Names Identified as Slavic but Labeled Greek - A Linguistic Challenge

Come take a ride in Tito's Time Machine

Declassified Documents 1939 to 1949

Dismantling the Greek Myth

Exhibition on the First Doctoral Dissertation on the Macedonian Language

From Macedonia to Australia

From Sanskrit to Macedonskrit

Greek names of Macedonian Village Names Changed by Greeks

Guilty Without Guilt

Herr Štefan Füle: EU Commissioner for European Neighbourhood Policy

History of the Macedonian People

History of the Macedonian People From Ancient times to the Present

HLA genes in Macedonians and the sub-Saharan origin of the Greeks

Holocaust of the Macedonian Jews

Macedonian Grammar 1952

Simon Tasievski

Inhabited Places In Aegean Macedonia

Justinian I The Great Macedonian Imperator Of Konstantinopolitana Nova Roma (Constantinople)

Lerin in mourning

Lexical Transference in the Speech of Macedonian English Bilingual Speakers in the Illawarra

Macedonia - What went wrong in the last 200 years

Macedonia Above All

Macedonia In Ancient Times

Macedonia The Land Of Legends

Macedonian Struggle For Independence

Macedonian village names that were changed

Macedonians In The World

Mincho Fotev and the Macedonian National Liberation Movement in Greece

Mystery Of Alexander's Grave

Our Macedonian Agenda

Prehistory Central Balkans

Prespa in Flames and Smoke

Proto Slavic Roots of the European Languages

Putting the Name Issue in a Comparative Perspective

Recovering Macedonia

Republic of Macedonia - Erga Omnes

Rosetta Stone 26-2-2005

Short History of the Macedonian People

Studies In The History Of Art VOL 10

The Ancient History of the Egyptians, Carthaginians, Assyrians, Babylonians, Medes and Persians, Macedonians and Grecians Volume 1 – 7

The Ancient Kingdom of Macedonia and the Republic of Macedonia

The Balkan Mega-Ethnos

The Centre Text On The Rosetta Stone

The Ethnic Minorities in Greece

The Great Lie

The Invention of the Slavic Fairytale

The Little Book Of Big Greek Lies

The Macedonian Genius Through The Centuries

The Macedonian Question 20 Years Of Political Struggle

The Name Game

The Other Face Of History

The Siege Of Svetigrad Saint City 1448

The Solun Assassins

The Terror In Aegean Macedonia Under Greek Occupation

To Hell And Back

Tracing the origins of the first Christian community in Europe - Macedonian Autocephalous Apostolic Church

Very Short History of the Macedonian People From Prehistory to the Present

Were There Any Slavs In Seventh Century Macedonia

Who Are The Modern Greeks

Why Macedonians WEREN'T Greek

Macedonia: A History

Simon Tasievski

www.ingramcontent.com/pod-product-compliance
Lightning Source LLC
Chambersburg PA
CBHW061734070526
44585CB00024B/2673